THE LEUENBERG
AGREEMENT AND
LUTHERAN–REFORMED
RELATIONSHIPS

THE LEUENBERG AGREEMENT AND LUTHERAN–REFORMED RELATIONSHIPS

Evaluations by North American and European Theologians

Edited by
William G. Rusch
and Daniel F. Martensen

Augsburg ▪ Minneapolis

THE LEUENBERG AGREEMENT AND LUTHERAN–REFORMED RELATIONSHIPS
Evaluations by North American and European Theologians

Scripture quotations unless otherwise noted are from the Revised Standard Version of the Bible, copyright 1946, 1952, and 1971 by the Division of Christian Education of the National Council of Churches.

The Leuenberg Agreement is reprinted by permission on pages 139-154 from *Lutheran World* 20 (1973): 347-53.

Library of Congress Cataloging-in-Publication Data

The Leuenberg Agreement and Lutheran–Reformed relationships / edited
  by William G. Rusch and Daniel F. Martensen.
     p.   cm.
    ISBN 0-8066-2436-1
    1. Reformatorische Kirchen und Ökumenische Bewegung. 2. Lutheran
Church—Relations—Reformed Church. 3. Reformed Church—Relations—
Lutheran Church. I. Rusch, William G. II. Martensen, Daniel F.
  BX8063.7.R4L47   1989
  280'.042—dc20   89-36050
                                                  CIP

The paper used in this publication meets the minimum requirements of American National Standard for Information Sciences—Permanence of Paper for Printed Library Materials, ANSI Z329.48-1984. ∞™

Manufactured in the U.S.A.   9-2436

93   92   91   90   89   1   2   3   4   5   6   7   8   9   10

Contents

Preface 7
    WILLIAM G. RUSCH AND DANIEL F. MARTENSEN

List of Participants 9

1 Background 11
    WILLIAM G. RUSCH

2 The Leuenberg Agreement: Origins and Aims 13
    MARC LIENHARD

3 The Leuenberg Agreement from 1973 to 1988 35
    ANDRÉ BIRMELÉ

4 Critique of the Leuenberg Agreement as an Ecumenical
    Model 53
    HARDING MEYER

5 An Evaluation of the Leuenberg Agreement: A Reformed
    Perspective 67
    PAUL R. FRIES

6   The Leuenberg Agreement in the North American
    Context 81
    WALTER SUNDBERG

7   The Leuenberg Agreement in the North American
    Context 97
    ROBERT JENSON

8   Ecumenical Perspectives on the Leuenberg Agreement .. 107
    ELISABETH SCHIEFFER

9   Observations by Other Lutheran Dialogue Partners 115
    GERALD MOEDE
    WILLIAM NORGREN
    GEORGE TAVARD

10 Summary Observations 123
    KARLFRIED FROELICH
    GABRIEL FACKRE

11 Reflections 133
    MARY B. HAVENS
    KEITH NICKLE

Appendix: The Leuenberg Agreement 139

Preface

The Constitution of the Evangelical Lutheran Church in America declares that the Office for Ecumenical Affairs shall encourage the study of theological topics and shall administer ecumenical dialogues (ELCA Constitution, chapter 16.21.A87, c and d). Lutheran–Reformed relationships is one of the areas in which the Office of Ecumenical Affairs does this work. The Constituting Convention of the Evangelical Lutheran Church in America specifically requested the newly merged church to be active in this area.

Today responsible ecumenical work needs to include a global awareness. The Leuenberg Agreement, developed in Europe in 1973, is one of the key documents that deals with Lutheran–Reformed relationships. Therefore, the Office for Ecumenical Affairs and the Institute for Ecumenical Research in Strasbourg (related to the Lutheran World Federation) cosponsored an international consultation on the Leuenberg Concord. This consultation had a twofold purpose to facilitate a better understanding of the Concord in the Evangelical Lutheran Church in America and to test the extent to which this European document is suitable to the American context.

This book is a record of that consultation. We hope that its publication will allow a larger audience, both in the Evangelical Lutheran Church in America and beyond, to share in its contributions and discussions. Thus, we are pleased to make this volume available as a resource for further reflection.

WILLIAM G. RUSCH
Executive Director
Office for Ecumenical Affairs

DANIEL F. MARTENSEN
Associate Director
Office for Ecumenical Affairs

List of Participants

André Birmelé	Professor, Institute for Ecumenical Research, Strasbourg, France
Gabriel Fackre	Professor, Andover Newton Theological School, Newton, Massachusetts, and member of the Lutheran–Reformed Committee for Theological Conversations
Paul R. Fries	Professor, New Brunswick Theological Seminary, New Jersey, and member of the Lutheran–Reformed Committee for Theological Conversations
Karlfried Froehlich	Professor, Princeton Theological Seminary, Princeton, member of the Lutheran–Roman Catholic Dialogue and the Lutheran–Reformed Committee for Theological Conversations
Mary B. Havens	Associate Professor, Lutheran Theological Seminary, Columbia, South Carolina, and Co-chairperson of the Lutheran–Reformed Committee for Theological Conversations

Robert Jenson	Professor, St. Olaf College, Northfield, Minnesota
Marc Lienhard	Professor, University of Strasbourg, France
Daniel F. Martensen	Associate Director, Evangelical Lutheran Church in America, Office for Ecumenical Affairs, Chicago, Illinois
Harding Meyer	Professor and Director, Institute for Ecumenical Research, Strasbourg, France
Gerald Moede	United Methodist Parish Pastor, Adell, Wisconsin, and former General Secretary of the Consultation on Church Union
Keith Nickle	Presbyterian Church Parish Pastor, Jefferson City, Tennessee, and Cochairperson of the Lutheran–Reformed Committee for Theological Conversations
William A. Norgren	Episcopal Church Ecumenical Officer, New York, New York, and Lutheran–Episcopal Dialogue Staff Person
William G. Rusch	Executive Director, Evangelical Lutheran Church in America, Office for Ecumenical Affairs, Chicago, Illinois
Elisabeth Schieffer	Docent, Heidelberg University, Federal Republic of Germany
Walter Sundberg	Associate Professor, Luther Northwestern Theological Seminary, St. Paul, Minnesota
George Tavard	Professor Emeritus, Methodist School of Theology, Columbus, Ohio, and member of the Lutheran–Roman Catholic Dialogue

1

Background

It is a well-known fact that Lutheran–Reformed relationships in the United States have been one of the most challenging areas of ecumenical activity—at least among Lutherans! The three merging churches of the Evangelical Lutheran Church in America (ELCA), for example, were at two different points at the time of merger. Thus, the responsibility to find a way into the future came to the ELCA. Building on the action of the Commission for a New Lutheran Church, the ELCA is doing several things. These include a series of theological conversations, the encouragement of joint study of the earlier dialogue reports, and the present study.

It might seem obvious that the Leuenberg Agreement holds a special place in Lutheran–Reformed relationships. Yet for American Lutherans, Leuenberg has been something of a puzzle. It has gained considerable support in many places in the world; but no U.S. church, Lutheran or Reformed, has adopted it. The second series of our dialogue in the U.S. did not even see it as a serious resource. The third series claimed to build its conclusions on it! Much of the literature on Leuenberg and its subsequent history is in German and not in English.

Thus, it seemed that to advance Lutheran–Reformed relations in this country, attention needed to be given to Leuenberg, not only its contents, but also its background and subsequent history. Therefore the Office for Ecumenical Affairs, acting with the Institute for Ecumenical Research at Strasbourg, an affiliate of the Lutheran World Federation, sponsored this consultation. The key persons in the story of Leuenberg participated in it, as did other recognized authorities. The U.S. members of the international Lutheran–Reformed dialogue, the members of the U.S. Lutheran–Reformed conversations, the Standing Committee of the Office for Ecumenical Affairs, the ELCA bishops committee on ecumenical relations, leadership from the three churches of the World Alliance of Reformed Churches, and other colleagues in the ecumenical movement were invited.

It was our expectation that those who participated would study the Leuenberg Agreement, learn from each other, and hear material that would become available in our churches. No formal, final report was planned, but we did decide to publish in this volume all the lectures at the consultation. Thus the work of those who spoke there can serve as a resource for the clergy of the ELCA.

I wish to express a word of sincere thanks to Professor Harding Meyer and his colleagues, who immediately saw the importance of this consultation and joined with us in every possible way to make this venture a success. Without their assistance, this event could not have happened, certainly not on this level.

My last word is one of thanks to all who came and gave their time. May the future of Lutheran–Reformed relationships prove that time well spent.

2

The Leuenberg Agreement: Origins and Aims

On 24 September 1971, an assembly of delegates from the Lutheran, Reformed, and United churches of Europe (as well as representatives of the Waldensians and of the Moravian Brothers) adopted a draft agreement which was to declare and realize fellowship between these different churches. After having received the reactions of the churches involved and after having modified the text accordingly, the final version was adopted on 16 March 1973 and submitted to the churches.[1] For the subscribing churches, fellowship was to come into effect on 1 October 1974. At the moment, about eighty churches have subscribed to it. There are also, among them, several non-European churches (essentially from South America).[2]

This chronology and these figures are, of course, only one aspect of this event or of this document known as the Leuenberg Agreement. The purpose of my lecture is to discuss three questions: first, what was the background of the Leuenberg Agreement; second, which method was followed to draw up the Agreement; and third, what is its content and its aim?

BACKGROUND

The Historical Situation

We must recall first of all that many Lutheran and Reformed churches of Europe live in close proximity to one another and have so for centuries.[3] This proximity is both geographic and confessional. In most cases except in Scandinavia, the Reformed partner feels close to the Lutheran partner (and vice versa), in particular when facing the Roman Catholic church or some of the free churches. In France, for instance, Lutheran pastors have been installed as pastors in Reformed congregations (and vice versa).

Particularly in the nineteenth and twentieth centuries, a number of factors have contributed to the reinforcement of the rapprochement and to putting confessional differences in perspective. In the nineteenth century, the same revival movements were experienced in the churches. The renewal of Bible studies, in particular the historical-critical approach, had a similar effect. These factors had led the churches "to new and similar ways of thinking and living" as is acknowledged in the Leuenberg Agreement (LA 5).

It is also fitting to recall the questions that challenged the European churches in the twentieth century:

- The confrontation of the German churches with Hitler's totalitarianism played a large role in this rapprochement. It even led to a common confession: the Barmen Confession. The impulse born out of this was still felt after 1945, in spite of certain divergences of opinion on the weight to be given to Barmen.[4]
- The challenge of secularization brought about considerable changes in the very life of the churches. As is found in the Schauenburg report published before the Leuenberg discussions: "In the practice of their Christian faith, Lutherans and Reformed differ less from one another now than in former days. Pastoral answers to questions of the time differ little one from the other. If they do differ, it is not because of confessional boundaries. The forms in which the life and the commitment of the parishes are translated are necessarily alike, even though forms of worship remain different by principle and in practice."[5]

Another factor of change is the mobility of the German population, which results in Protestants passing without any difficulty from a Lutheran church to a Reformed or a United one. Hence, the awareness of *belonging to a* confessional tradition (i.e., Lutheran or Reformed) has weakened quite a bit among the faithful—and among many pastors. Even before the Leuenberg Agreement, intercommunion was practiced in countries like France or Austria.

Lastly, let us note the impact of the ecumenical movement and the importance of the universality of the Church in contact with the young churches. For the young churches, most often confronting a majority of non-Christians, confessional differences inherited from the past and from Europe have been toned down. These churches have sought to deepen their communion and their common witness. This, of course, was a direct challenge for the churches of Europe. Also, involved in the ecumenical movement, confronted since Vatican II by certain changes in the Roman Catholic church, and brought to confess a common faith with churches of very different traditions (see the Lima document), the Lutheran and Reformed churches have been led to reconsider their inherited divisions.

The observations we have just voiced have, for the most part, remained on the level of simple empirical, even sociological findings. Such an approach is limited, for two reasons. On the one hand, similar but opposite observations could also be drawn from this simple, empirical level. We could note, for example, the nineteenth-century rise of Neo-Lutheranism which laid much emphasis on the sixteenth-century confessions of faith and on the identity of the Lutheran church. In the twentieth century, one effect of the ecumenical dialogue has been to favor building awareness of what confessional identity signifies. However, differences still manifest themselves, in particular when it comes to worship: many Lutherans feel closer to the Anglican tradition, whereas the Reformed often feel closer to the free churches. Differences in the organization of the churches could also be mentioned.

Theological Dialogue

On the other hand, it is also not enough to note that on the level of what is experienced, there is a concrete rapprochement between the Lutheran and the Reformed churches. Questions also must be asked on the traditional theological level, as expressed in the sixteenth century confessions of faith that are still in use in most of the Lutheran[6] and Reformed churches. How are we to evaluate these traditional differences nowadays? How can we overcome them in a dialogue that takes into account the present day teaching of the churches? How are we able to integrate them in a church fellowship based on a clear theological vision?

Such were the questions debated during the many theological dialogues which, between 1945 and 1970, paved the way in Europe for the Leuenberg Agreement.[7] The Agreement, realized between 1969 and 1973, would not have been possible without this background, which was both regional or national, and European.

Before we deal with the Agreement itself, let us take a brief look at the main aspects of this background. In Germany, a dialogue carried out over nearly ten years, and based mostly on a biblical and exegetical approach, culminated in 1957 in the famous Arnoldshain theses, which discuss the Lord's Supper and link the imparting of Christ's body and blood to the bread and wine.[8] In 1956, the same subject had been discussed in ten theses in the Netherlands.[9] In France, a similar dialogue led, in 1964, to theses on the Word of God and the Holy Scripture, baptism, and the Lord's Supper, also expressing a notable agreement.[10] An agreement of a more general nature, formulated in 1959 in West Germany, had concluded that confessional differences would no longer justify the separation of the churches.[11] In 1969 and in 1970, several dialogues also took place in both Germanies.[12]

In 1955, a dialogue between the Lutherans and the Reformed was also begun on a European level.[13] It dealt successively with the question of the authority of Holy Scripture (1957), the presence of Christ (1958), baptism (1959), and the Lord's Supper (1960). However, even if a rapprochement of points of views seemed to emerge, these dialogues did not issue any elaborate declarations. The Schauenburg talks (1964–1967)[14] proved different. This was sort of a midway point between the former dialogues, which dealt with specific subjects such as the Lord's Supper, and the Leuenberg approach, which set a wider framework based on a particular vision of church fellowship. At the same time, dialogues on theological points yet insufficiently studied, were carried out, leading to theses on "Word of God and presence of God" (1964), "the law" (1965), and "the confession of faith." What was stated is that the differences which separate the Lutheran and the Reformed churches have disclosed themselves as oppositions within a common space, a space such as does not exist in the same way between other churches.[15]

The evolution thus started culminated in the dialogue that took place in Leuenberg from 1969 to 1973.[16] The concentration on church fellowship was striking. The question asked was to what extent the assent on central doctrinal points (the understanding of the gospel, baptism, the Lord's Supper, Christology) that was supposed to have been reached through the former dialogues could be the basis for a true church fellowship between the involved churches.

In a report issued at Leuenberg in 1970,[17] this fellowship is rooted in the acknowledgment of the exclusive mediation of Jesus Christ for our salvation—an affirmation recognized as the "heart" and core of the gospel[18] and the only foundation and rule of the doctrine and life of the church. From that basis, the doctrine of justification by faith and of the new birth was to be developed, and also the realization of an agreement on the accomplishment of the Word and the sacraments.

The report ends on a proposal to implement church fellowship through an agreement submitted for approval to the churches. This agreement was to be made up of three sections:

- a declaration expressing the agreement of the churches in their understanding of the gospel's content;
- a declaration affirming that the condemnations expressed in the confessions of faith do not concern the partner today and that the differences remaining in the doctrine, the institutions and the styles of church life no longer prevent fellowship between the churches;
- a declaration proclaiming pulpit and altar fellowship in the churches involved.

A draft agreement adopted in 1971 was then sent to the churches for examination. The final text was adopted on 16 March 1973.[19]

METHOD

Before studying the text, I would like in this second section to discuss two major questions that derive from the approach that led to Leuenberg.

The Concept of Agreement (Konkordie)

This concept, suggested by Peter Brunner and Joachim Staedtke, goes back to the sixteenth century. The most famous example is the Wittenberg Agreement realized in 1536 between the Wittenberg theologians, on the one hand, and the theologians of Upper Germany (Bucer), on the other.[20] Following the insight of Ireneus, this Agreement saw in the Lord's Supper a heavenly reality and an earthly reality. Thus, clearly rejecting both transubstantiation and the local inclusion of the body and blood of Christ in the elements, the Agreement stated: "In virtue of the sacramental union the bread is the body of Christ, that is . . . when the bread is offered the body of Christ is present at the same time and truly offered."[21] Note that, at the time, one spoke of the communion of the unworthy, namely, the believers! Thus, in Luther's eyes, a certain objectivity was preserved concerning the gift of Christ, whose reality was not to depend on the condition of the human soul. Luther himself went even further, teaching the manducation of the ungodly, that is the nonbelievers. What is to be remembered is that the agreement did not erase certain differences existing between both parties. It did not become a Lutheran confession of faith (even though it is included in the Book of Concord).[22] According to certain recent interpretations, it would in fact only be a declaration by theologians of Upper Germany acknowledged by the theologians of Wittenberg who were there as witnesses.

However, this agreement allowed what Marburg did not make possible between Zwingli and Luther. In 1536, the representatives of both parties communed together. And the Wittenberg Agreement marked the beginning of a lasting rapprochement between the churches of Saxony and those of Upper Germany—in spite of differences remaining, for instance, between the theology of Bucer (and of the Strasbourg theologians) and the theology of Luther[23], or certain differences in forms of church life.

Thus, if in the twentieth century the concept and idea of an Agreement is picked up anew, it is to distinguish the assent sought out from a confession of faith common to both, since Lutherans and Reformed do not have quite the same understanding of the hermeneutical role of a confession.[24] Hence, it is neither useful nor desirable to seek out an agreement that would be understood as a common confession of faith. For, in order to realize church fellowship according to article 7 of the Augsburg Confession, "it is enough to agree concerning the teaching of the gospel and the administration of the sacraments" (Latin text).

The Leuenberg Agreement was intended to express such a consensus, which would not have the status of a confession of faith. It would be understood, according to the terms used by Staedtke, "as a doctrinal agreement *(Vereinbarung)* which does try to express the gospel of the grace of God in an integral way, but does not take into account the diversity of the theological, political and historical conditions to which the various churches are submitted."[25] Thus the Agreement was not intended to *substitute* for the confessions of faith of these churches. These confessions were to retain their authority as hermeneutical key for the reading of the Scripture and norm for preaching today. But within this process, confessions must be interpreted. The assent obtained through the agreement marks one phase in such a process of interpretation.

Consensus

The authors of the Leuenberg Agreement were convinced of the importance of theological dialogue to generate church fellowship. This same approach had been adopted in the sixteenth century to produce the Wittenberg Agreement and other similar texts. The Leuenberg Agreement saw light because of the conviction that it does not suffice to work together as churches and even that it does not suffice to proclaim, in fact, the same gospel. There was the conviction that this fact also had to be expressed by a doctrinal consensus which was a commitment on the part of the churches involved. To recognize and to express together the truth of faith is a fundamental moment on the way leading to unity.

One could think, however, that in view of the present day pluralism of worship, of philosophic divergences, and of language problems, the production of such an Agreement had become more difficult now than in the sixteenth century. Yet, the attempt was made in Leuenberg because of the conviction that there is more than the preaching of the gospel, because of the conviction that there is also the church, which expresses this gospel, and gathers round it.

One of the characteristics of the Leuenberg approach is the concentration on what is, according to Article 7 of the Augsburg Confession, the criterion for church fellowship, namely, the assent over the proclamation of the gospel. Whereas former dialogues had elaborated often lengthy theses on subjects such as the Lord's Supper or the confession of faith, there was in Leuenberg an obvious effort to concentrate on what was called in the Agreement "the heart of the Scriptures" (article 12) or in preparatory texts, the "foundation." In this perspective, we must distinguish the "heart" or the core from the periphery or consequences, the basis from the expressions of this basis, the foundation from the traditions, or the *fides justificans* from the *fides dogmatica*." This was, according to the authors of the Leuenberg Agreement, a way of applying article 7 of the Augsburg Confession to doctrine. The common foundation was that on which the church was founded, namely the very gospel, in distinction from historical traditions, including doctrinal ones, which do not, in an absolute way, require a consensus. In this perspective, church fellowship is not based on an agreement on the whole of a creed anymore, but on what is the foundation of church unity, namely that "it is enough to agree concerning the teaching of the gospel and the administration of the sacraments" (Augsburg Confession, article 7, Latin text).

This distinction between consensus over the gospel, defined more precisely as message of the justification, and "human traditions," as doctrines expressive of the foundation, prompted criticisms, of course, in particular on the part of the Finnish theologian Mannermaa.[26] He drew attention to the fact that, according to this logic, the greater part of the Augsburg Confession is liable to become secondary since it is only the clarification of justification itself. But the question remains in the Augsburg Confession to know whether everything must be put on the same level and make church fellowship depend on the adoption of the whole of this confession, or whether it is possible and necessary to bring out the core of this confession which determines the whole.

Also, if the common basis that is the message of salvation in Jesus Christ, expressed in a central way by the affirmation of justification by faith, is stressed, then one does not remain on the level of the Agreement but is directed to the undergirding consensus. The idea is also to show that the central message, thus understood and on which there is assent, determines the understanding and the practice of the sacraments, another criterion for church fellowship. The message of justification by faith implies that God really gives what God promises through the Word, namely the body and blood of Christ given for the sinner. Christ is my righteousness before God and this Christ must really be given for me. This is done through the preaching of the Word and through the sacraments. The saving presence of Christ cannot be beyond that and we do not receive forgiveness independently from these means of salvation. It must also be clear that the saving gift is not prompted by faith but received by faith. If there is assent on this subject—and I believe that the Leuenberg Agreement expresses this assent—then there are no more obstacles to church fellowship.

But once we admit there is an assent over the "heart of the Scripture" and its concretization in the sacraments, then what becomes of the traditional theological differences between the Lutherans and the Reformed? I would make three remarks on that subject:

■ First, the central message pertaining to the gospel and the sacraments may be founded or expounded in various ways at the christological and ontological levels. Thus, for instance, the true presence of Christ in the Lord's Supper has often been based, for the Lutherans, on the doctrine of ubiquity. But that is not the only way to do it, even in the Lutheran tradition. It is a possible expression of the faith, but cannot be laid down as a doctrine that must absolutely be accepted for the realization of church fellowship.

- Second, the authors of the Leuenberg Agreement feel that theological divergences that do not have to do with the very basis of the "hearts" can and must be examined and eventually overcome within the very framework of church fellowship. Thus Wenzel Lohff was able to say that "the consensus over the foundation which is the *doctrina evangelii* was the prolepsis used to do away with doctrinal differences."[27]

- Third, it is important to draw attention to the following fact. Within the framework of church fellowship, an assent over the "heart," over the core, does not exclude different emphases. There need not be a static and harmonious complementarity; there can be reciprocal and permanent questioning. As an example, it is clear that the Reformed tradition placed emphasis on sanctification derived from the acceptance by God of the sinner. The Lutheran tradition, on the other hand, stressed faith as the prerequisite to this acceptance, sanctification as the fruit, and the freedom existing in Christian life.

CONTENT AND AIM OF THE LEUENBERG AGREEMENT

It is not possible within the framework of this lecture to present a thorough analysis of the whole text. I will limit myself to expanding the most prominent points.

I shall start with the structure. Besides the preamble, the Agreement is made up of four parts: The first section is entitled "The Road to Fellowship." It recalls the divisions of the sixteenth century and then speaks of "the common elements in the witness of the churches" at the outset of the Reformation, followed by the changed presuppositions in the contemporary church situation. The second section is entitled "The Common Understanding of the Gospel" and speaks of justification as "the message of the free grace of God," then of preaching, of Baptism, and of the Lord's Supper. A third section expands on the "Accord in Respect of the Doctrinal Condemnations of the Reformation Era," namely the Lord's Supper, Christology, and predestination. Finally a fourth section deals with "The Declaration and Realization of Church Fellowship."

The Reformation Heritage

Note how often, mostly but not exclusively in the first section, the Leuenberg Agreement refers to history and in particular to the sixteenth century Reformation.

In the preamble, mention is made of the criteria set by the Reformers (for instance article 7 of the Augsburg Confession) for the establishment of church fellowship. In the Agreement, several references are made to the sixteenth century confessions of faith. In Section III particularly, the need to overcome the condemnations pronounced in these confessions against the Reformed or Lutheran partner is underlined. In Section IV also, this concern is mentioned by pointing to the fact that confessions remain in use. Concerning the sixteenth century, the Agreement avoids speaking of a common starting point (*Ansatz*) between Lutherans and Reformed, partly because of a study by Jean-Louis Leuba.[28] This author felt that the starting point for the Lutherans had been justification by faith, whereas for the Reformed, it was the authority of the Scripture alone compared with human traditions. However, the Leuenberg Agreement refers to a certain number of "common elements in the witness of the churches of the reformation" (LA 3). In the name of the same reference to the gospel, they "found themselves drawn together in opposition to the church traditions of that time," they affirmed the normative authority of Holy Scripture for life and faith, and bore "witness to God's free and unconditional grace in the life, death and resurrection of Jesus Christ" (4).

The Reformation is not an absolute novelty, because the churches born of the Reformation "renewed their confession with the whole of Christendom, the faith as expressed in the ancient creeds of the church" (4). In spite of their closeness, they were not able to avoid divisions. According to the Agreement, these were due to "real differences in style of theological thinking and church practice" (3).

The text could of course not go into details. But this brings to mind the localization of the risen Christ's body by Zwingli, for instance, or the ontological implications of the *communicatio idiomatum* doctrine.[29] Then there is mention of the history following that period. Indeed, the confessions of faith of the sixteenth century are still valid and Lutherans stress that quite strongly.

It is, however, impossible to act as if Lutherans and Reformed were still at the same point as at Marburg in 1529, or at Wittenberg in 1536. As Leonhard Goppelt said, "Partners have changed because of a history of four hundred years, changed from what they were in the sixteenth century, and from what they were at the beginning of the twentieth century." This changing is not apostasy, and more than an evolution or a change in the history of ideas. In a Johannine perspective, it means being led further "into all the truth" (John 16:13).[30] The Agreement mentions some of the aspects of this history, in particular the evolution of biblical research. The conclusion drawn from all this is important for the manner in which sixteenth century confessions of faith are received nowadays. As the first version of the Agreement said, the task is not to "take them up under a new expression." "The fundamental witness" of the confessions must be distinguished from "historically conditioned thought forms" (5).

The Agreement continues: "Because" [*quia* and not *quantenus*!] these confessions of faith bear witness to the gospel as the living word of God in Jesus Christ, far from barring the way to continued responsible testimony of the Word, they open up this way with a call to follow it in the freedom of faith" (5).

The Gospel: Foundation for Church Fellowship

The second section of the Agreement expresses the common understanding of the gospel, not in an exhaustive way, but insofar as this is required for establishing church fellowship between the churches involved.

The distinction is made between the message as such, called the "message of justification as message of the free grace of God," and the forms in which this message is transmitted, namely preaching, Baptism, and the Lord's Supper. Let us point to some of the important aspects. First we note the stress upon the Christological content of the gospel as "the message of Jesus Christ, the salvation of the world" (7). Thus, it should be noticed, the gospel is not only expressed as justification by faith; although the doctrine of justification is a normative way in which to express "the true understanding of the gospel" (8). Let us also note the joint affirmation of justification and sanctification. "God assures the believing sinner of his righteousness in Jesus Christ" (10). This is a concise formulation to express justification by faith. Light is also shed on this by the mention of the "setting free from the accusation of the law." The Christian thus freed is called to daily repentance and renewal, praise of God and in service to others. That is sanctification.

In conformity with the orientation of the confessions of faith of the Reformation, the Agreement stresses "service in the world," in particular in standing up for peace. Lastly, the final version of the Agreement declares that "we take our stand on the basis of the ancient creeds of the church" (12). It is out of the question to confine oneself to a Protestantism which would believe that nothing happened between biblical days and the sixteenth century!

The second part of section two deals with the subjects of preaching, baptism and the Lord's Supper. Concerning the place and the importance of preaching, there was of course no disagreement. The final version of the Agreement has also included a remark on ministry: "The Lord employs various forms of ministry and service as well as the witness of all those belonging to his people" (13). There is some difference between the Lutheran tradition, which places emphasis on the one form of ordained ministry, and the Reformed tradition, which is attached to more than one form of ministry. The Agreement seems to tend toward that latter direction. What is important is to underline that differences concerning ministry and the structure of the churches were not considered in the sixteenth century as an obstacle to church fellowship.

The same can be said about baptism. A difference had appeared in the sixteenth century between the Reformed tradition, which allocates to baptism a significant role (salvation through Jesus Christ is made known to the baptized person), and the Lutheran tradition, which stresses the efficient action of baptism. God acts through baptism. The Agreement states that "in baptism, Jesus Christ irrevocably receives man, fallen prey to sin . . . into his fellowship of salvation" (14). "Irrevocably" does not, of course, signify that the baptized person is saved once and for all. It means that God's faithfulness to the promise in baptism remains, even if the baptized person drifts away from the covenant of salvation. The idea is to react against a depreciation of infant baptism.

The statements on the Lord's Supper are connected to the Arnoldshain theses, but shorter.

The point is less a description of the Lord's Supper as such, than the statement, in soteriological terms, of how Christ acts toward us, within this framework. He "imparts himself . . . he grants us . . . ," etc. (15).

As in the Arnoldshain theses and as in the American theses of *Marburg Revisited*[31] (which also spoke of the Holy Spirit), the Leuenberg Agreement places emphasis on the Word. The elements are instruments of Christ and "his word of promise" (15). There remains a certain amount of disagreement in as much as the Lutherans will speak of consecration, something which the Reformed generally refuse to do. Whatever the case, the word is more than word of information. It is truly part of the acting of Christ in the sacrament.

"Christ imparts himself in his body and blood" (15). Two possible false interpretations must be avoided here: on the one hand, the concept that would isolate the body and blood of Christ from the person of Christ and would make him a sort of "celestial matter"; on the other hand, a spiritualist or docetist concept that would reduce the person to his spirit. The one who gives himself is Jesus Christ, as he suffered for us, namely in his body and in his blood. The risen one is no other but the crucified, even if now his body is glorified.

As in most of the other Lutheran and Reformed theses, the *"cum"* of the Wittenberg Agreement (1536)[32] was used here also, to express the link between Christ and the elements. As is stated in the official explanation of the Arnoldshain theses:

"The subscribers have renounced trying to specify more extensively the link existing between body and blood of Christ and bread and wine, out of consideration for the plurality of witness in the New Testament."

For Lutherans, the main point is stated, namely that the gift of bread and wine and the gift of body and blood of Christ are not two separate actions but are identified. The Leuenberg Agreement states this clearly when it says (while discussing the condemnations pronounced against views of the Lord's Supper) that "we cannot separate communion with Jesus Christ in his body and blood from the act of eating and drinking" (19).

To stress the objectivity of the real presence and of the gift of Christ, Luther spoke of the *"manducatio impiorum,"* stating that even the nonbelievers received the body and the blood of Christ. Bucer accepted only the *"manducatio indignorum,"* aiming at believers whose faith was weak. The Agreement deals with this point also, in the part on condemnations (19). It states that Christ "gives himself unreservedly to all who receive the bread and wine" (18). But we could ask: "Does everyone receive him?" The next part of the text deals with that. "Faith receives the Lord's Supper for salvation, unfaith for judgment." Contrary to certain suspicions on the part of the Lutherans, what was really meant was that it is Christ who is received in both cases, and not only the bread and the wine.

The trend in the sixteenth century was often to concentrate on the controversial question of the mode of presence of Christ, or to express the fruits of the Lord's Supper in an excessively individualistic way (forgiveness of sins, life, salvation). Twentieth century exegesis has led to the development of other perspectives, in particular the link between sacrament and ethics, the dimension of community, and the eschatological orientation. This can be found in the Agreement (11).

Beyond Condemnations

The third section deals with the doctrinal condemnations pronounced in the Reformation era.

According to the sixteenth century confessions of both the Reformed and Lutheran churches, certain doctrines of the other are not simply the result of an inevitable pluralism, as one would tend to say nowadays, but of another gospel. Thus very strong condemnations have been pronounced (for instance in Article 10 of the Augsburg Confession, concerning the Lord's Supper), against the opposite doctrine, and even against "those who teach differently." These condemnations relate to three specific points: the Lord's Supper, Christology, and predestination.[33] Although the Lutherans issued such condemnations in a clearer manner than the Reformed, equivalent passages can be found in the Reformed confessions. The impact of these condemnations was clear in the sixteenth century: church fellowship was made impossible. At the end of his life, Luther still applied to the successors of Zwingli the words of the apostle: "As for a man who is factious, . . . have nothing more to do with him" (Titus 3:10).[34]

Let us note that in the ecumenical movement nowadays, the question of condemnations of the sixteenth century exists also in relationships with other churches. In 1980, during the anniversary of the Augsburg Confession, the Mennonites brought up the question of the condemnations—at least five!—stated in the Augsburg Confession concerning the Anabaptists and their doctrines. Since 1980, several groups have set to work on this question, to examine the present impact of these condemnations on the relationships between Lutherans and Mennonites[35] and between Lutherans and Baptists. The same kind of work is being done at the level of the Lutheran–Roman Catholic dialogue and was discussed in a recent publication.[36]

How are condemnations expressed in the past expected to be overcome? The point is not to claim that our ancestors were mistaken in their condemnations, as if they could not distinguish truth from heresy. The point is to discover whether these condemnations still refer to something, namely, if they still concern the partner involved. This is a central point concerning the continuity and the identity of a confessional family. The possibility or the reality of a certain change, due in particular to a new reading of the Bible and to cultural changes, must be taken into account. Even if we remain true to the central aims of the sixteenth century confessions of faith, we express them differently today.

The Leuenberg Agreement thus became a sort of clarification: How do we understand the gospel today? How do we understand the ways in which the gospel expresses itself today? The Reformed who subscribed to the Leuenberg Agreement placed themselves beyond certain of Zwingli's conceptions (Lord's Supper as simple commemoration, location of Christ in heaven, and so forth) and even beyond certain of Calvin's, since double predestination was not mentioned anymore (under the influence of Barth, among others). As for the Lutherans, they were able to recognize, while still emphasizing the unity of the person of Christ, that the distinction between both natures of Christ had to be taken into more account (along with the Reformed tradition), this in order not to interfere with the humanity of Christ. Such had been the risk run by certain christological approaches in the sixteenth century *(communicatio idiomatum, genus majestaticum).* [37] While still keeping its basic statements (on incarnation, and so on), each church has thus found itself confronted with the failure of "traditional thought forms" (LA 22).

And so the *third section* of the Agreement states that whatever their historical importance or present usefulness, "the condemnations pronounced by the Reformation fathers, . . . are no longer an obstacle to church fellowship" (27). Also, "considerable differences . . . in spirituality and church order" remain but, "in fidelity to the New Testament and Reformation criteria," these do not seem to be "factors which should divide the church" (28).

Church Fellowship

I will speak more briefly concerning the theme of the fourth section, since a lecture on church fellowship has been scheduled. Note that this section distinguishes between the "declaration" and the "realization" of church fellowship. The former is implemented through the signing of the Agreement, the latter is a process set within the course of time and which achieves actual fellowship in the life of the churches.

The declaration of church fellowship reaffirms the agreement on the gospel developed in the second section, and recalls that the condemnations expressed in the confessions of faith "no longer apply to the contemporary doctrinal position of the assenting churches" (32). Paragraph 33 lists the concrete consequences of the declaration: that the churches concerned accord each other pulpit and altar fellowship; and that this implies the recognition of ordination and the freedom to provide for intercelebration.

What does this entail? First of all, that one of the churches involved cannot write by-laws that would forbid a pastor from another church, subscribing to the Agreement, to come and preside over worship in that particular church. This church remains, however, free to set its own rules on ways and means to celebrate worship (in particular concerning the liturgy). Also, the rights of pastors to concretely examine and decide who they will allow to preside over worship in their parishes is not challenged.

Mention is also made of the mutual recognition of ordination. If a pastor goes from one church to another, ordination is not repeated; different practical modalities belong to a legitimate diversity, and assent to the gospel has been acknowledged by the Leuenberg Agreement. It is not forbidden, however, for a particular church to request that a pastor accept the specific confessions of faith of the church in which the pastor wants to exercise the pastoral ministry. Indeed, the Leuenberg Agreement has not taken the place of these confessions of faith.

The Agreement leaves intact the binding force of the confessions within the participating churches. It is not to be regarded as a new confession of faith. It sets forth a consensus reached about central matters; one which makes church fellowship possible between churches of different confessional positions (37).

"Recognition of ordination does not affect the rules in force in the participating churches for induction to a pastoral charge and the exercise of the pastoral ministry" (43).

There could be a certain tension between the Agreement, which was intended only as a consensus sufficing for church fellowship, but which has, however, a confessing nature; and the affirmation of an unchanged validity of the traditional confessions of faith. Concerning "altar fellowship," it is generally understood as an open fellowship, an already widespread practice. Intercelebration is foreseen as a possibility. Concelebration should not give rise to any difficulty. However, it could happen that a Reformed pastor would have hesitations about celebrating the Lord's Supper following the Lutheran liturgy; that a Lutheran pastor would hesitate to follow the Reformed liturgy.

Finally, in the Federal Republic of Germany the Leuenberg Agreement was also experienced as a clarification concerning the question of church membership. Since 1970, it had been stipulated in the Evangelical Church of Germany (bringing together several different individual churches of the Federal Republic of Germany) that a believer moving to a different area would automatically become the member of the evangelical church of the territory on which he established himself. It was possible to decide that the Leuenberg Agreement furnished a theological basis for such an approach.

In the German Democratic Republic, the Leuenberg Agreement affected the different churches working together on a national level by strengthening their close association.

These few remarks have led us straight into a topic that is not ours to deal with: the realization of church fellowship. That topic involves both the history of the reception of the Leuenberg Agreement and the effort to translate the Agreement at the level of life together: either to overcome differences that are still obvious, or to integrate them clearly in church fellowship as a legitimate diversity of the body of Christ.

Notes

1. English text is published in *An Invitation to Action, The Lutheran–Reformed Dialogue. Series III 1981-1983*, ed. J. E. Andrews and J. A. Burgess (Fortress Press, Philadelphia, 1984). Appendix II, 61ff. (Reprinted in this volume, 139-154.)

2. See the list in André Birmelé, ed., *Konkordie und Ökumene. Die Leuenberger Kirchengemeinschaft in der gegenwärtigen ökumenischen Situation* (Francfort/Main, 1988), 171-173.

3. Concerning this question see the so-called report of Schauenburg: "Lutherische und Reformierte Kirchen in Europa auf dem Weg zueinander," in: *Auf dem Weg. Lutherisch–reformierte Kirchengemeinschaft*, Zurich, 1967 (= Polis 33), 9-43; French version: *Verbum Caro* 83 (1967): 29-65. (Hereafter cited as *Auf dem Weg*.)

4. See: *Die lutherischen Kirchen und die Bekenntnissynode von Barmen. Referate des Internationalen Symposiums auf der Reisenburg 1984*, published by W. D. Hauschild (Göttingen, 1984).

5. Schauenberg, III, 2. Text in *Auf dem Weg*, I: *Lutherisch–reformierte Kirchengemeinschaft* (Zurich: EV2 Verlag, 1967), 16-17.

6. The General Regulation of the Church of the Augsburg Confession of Alsace and Lorraine, worked out in 1988-89, affirms in its preamble that this church "is based on the Gospel of Jesus Christ attested by the Holy Scripture. The latter is the basic authority. In order to confess the centre of the Scripture and to gather the Church around the same confession of faith the ECAAL refers also to the symbols of the Ancient Church, to the Augsburg Confession and to Luther's Small Catechism."

7. See my book: *Lutherisch-reformierte Kirchengemeinschaft heute. Der Leuenberger Konkordienentwurf im Kontext der bisherigen lutherisch–reformierten Dialoge* (Francfort/Main, 1972, 2nd ed. 1973); (Hereafter cited as Lutherisch-Reformierte Kirchengemeinschaft.) and: Elisabeth Schieffer, *Von Schauenburg nach Leuenberg. Entstehung und Bedeutung der Konkordie reformatorischer Kirchen in Europa* (Paderborn, 1983). (Hereafter cited as *Von Schauenburg nach Leuenberg*.)

8. German text in *Von Schauenburg nach Leuenberg*, A5-6.

9. Ibid., 426-429.

10. *Recherches ecclésiales* 4 (1981): 8-16; in German: *Auf dem Weg*, 93-109.

11. Text in: *Auf dem Weg*, 66-92.

12. See the references and a summary in my book: *Lutherisch–reformierte Kirchengemeinschaft*, 20-25.

13. *Ibid.* 30ff; *Schieffer, Von Schauenburg nach Leuenberg*, 45-236.

14. See note 3.

15. Schauenburg, IV, 1. Text in *Auf dem Weg*.

16. See M. Lienhard's and E. Schieffer's books mentioned in note 7.

17. *Auf dem Weg* II (Zurich: 1971), 8-24.

18. The Leuenberg Agreement (12) would later speak more adequately of the "heart of the Scripture."

19. See note 1.

20. The most recent edition is to be found in *Bucers Deutsche Schriften* vol. 6, 1 (Gütersloh: 1988), 114-134.

21. *Ibid.* 122.

22. In the *Solidi Declaration* of the Formula of Concord, Article 7; in *The Book of Concord. The Confessions of the Evangelical Lutheran Church*, ed. Theodore Tappert (Philadelphia: Fortress Press, 1959), 571f.

23. See Ernst Bizer, *Studien zur Geschichte des Abendmahlsstreits im 16. Jahrhundert* (1940) (Gütersloh, 1962); W. Kohler, Zwingli und Luther, II (Gütersloh, 1953).

24. See Jean-Louis Leuba, "Die Union als ökumenisch-theologisches Problem," In: *Um evangelische Einheit. Beiträge zum Unionsproblem*, publ. by K. Herbert, Herborn, 1967, 290-324. Lienhard, *Lutherisch–reformierte Kirchengemeinschaft*, 45-47.

25. Joachim Staedtke, "Die Entstehung der innerprotestantischen Kirchentrennung," *Ökumenische Rundschau* 19 (1970), 25.

26. Tuomo Mannermaa, *Von Preussen nach Leuenberg. Hintergrund und Entwicklung der theologischen Methode in der Leuenberger Konkordie* (Hamburg: 1982). (= Arbeiten zur Geschichte und Theologie des Luthertums, Neue Folge vol. I.)

27. Wenzel Lohff, "Grund und Grenze der Kirche. Von der Bedeutung des Augsburgischen Bekenntnisses für das Bemühen von Kirchengemeinschaft im deutschen Protestantismus," *Evangelische Kommentare* 3 (1970); 16.

28. See footnote 24.

29. See my book, *Luther, témoin de Jésus-Christ. Les étapes et les thèmes de la christologie du Réformateur* (Paris: 1973); in English: *Luther: Witness to Jesus Christ. Stages and Themes of the Reformer's Christology* (Minneapolis: Augsburg Publishing House, 1982).

30. See the typed text of a lecture given in 1971; quoted in *Lienhard, Lutherisch–reformierte Kirchengemeinschaft*, 55.

31. *Marburg Revisited: A Reexamination of Lutheran and Reformed Traditions*, 3rd ed. (Minneapolis: Augsburg Publishing House, 1967).

32. Martin Bucers Deutsche Schriften, VI. 1: 120.

33. *Ibid.* 11. See my study: *Die Verwerfung der Irrlehre und das Verhältnis zwischen lutherischen und reformierten Kirchen.* In: *Auf dem Weg* II, p. 69-152.

34. WA 54, 142, 17.

35. *Les entretiens luthéro-mennonites. Les résultats du colloque de Strasbourg* (1981-1984), publ. by M. Lienhard and P. Widmer (= Les Cahiers de Christ seul; no. 16, no. spécial), Montbéliard, July 1984; M. Lienhard, Von der Konfrontation zum Dialog: Die lutherischen Kirchen und die Täufer im 16. Jahrhundert; in *Einheit der Kirche. Neue Entwicklungen und Perspektiven*, publ. by G. Gassmann and P. Højen, (Francfort/Main: 1988), 25-38.

36. K. Lehmann - W. Pannenberg, *Lehrverurteilungen - kirchentrennend?* I - *Rechtfertigung, Sakramente und Amt im Zeitalter der Reformation und heute*, Fribourg, 1986.

37. See my book: *Luther témoin de Jésus-Christ*, 234, 356-359; Luther: Witness to Jesus Christ, 225, 344-345.

ANDRÉ BIRMELÉ

3

The Leuenberg Agreement from 1973 to 1988

The purpose of this paper is to report on the main developments that have characterized church fellowship among the Lutheran, Reformed, and Union churches in Europe after the drafting of the Leuenberg Agreement in 1973. I shall address three areas: the complementary nature of the declaration and the realization of church fellowship, the continuation of theological dialogue, and the process of broader ecumenical reflection. Then I will offer an evaluation and some perspectives on the issues involved.

THE DECLARATION AND THE REALIZATION OF CHURCH FELLOWSHIP

The Starting Point

In the preparatory discussions that led to the drafting of the Leuenberg Agreement, the distinction suggested in Article 7 of the Augsburg Confession played a leading role. The article distinguished between what is necessary for the true unity of the church and what diversity is not only legitimate but also desirable. "For the true unity of the church, it is enough to agree concerning the teaching of the gospel and the administration of the sacraments. It is not necessary that human traditions or rites and ceremonies instituted by men should be alike everywhere" (Augsburg Confession 7). The Lutheran and Reformed churches of Europe adopted this perspective as the basis for their model of unity: it is necessary to seek a consensus in the understanding of Word and sacrament. When this understanding emerges, it will suffice for the establishment of church fellowship.[1]

The structure of the text of the Agreement expresses this idea of unity. After an introductory section dealing with the prerequisites for church fellowship, the common horizon of the churches born of the sixteenth century Reformation, and recent developments, the second section of the text expands on the "common understanding of the gospel" (LA 6-16). This section concentrates on "the message of justification as the message of the free grace of God." Church fellowship is based on a consensus in an understanding of the gospel, the grace of God, witnessed to and given by the word in preaching, by baptism and by the Lord's Supper (13 to 16). The understanding of the sacraments, especially the Lord's Supper, was debated and gave rise in the sixteenth century to reciprocal doctrinal condemnations. The authors made a point in the third section of showing that the sixteenth century doctrinal condemnations, about the Lord's Supper as well as Christology and predestination, indeed keep their theological merits but do not apply to the current doctrine of the sister churches. In light of recent developments, "it is impossible for us to reaffirm the former condemnations" (23, cf. 20, 26). Against this background, the Agreement's authors then propose in the fourth and last section to move on to the declaration and realization of church fellowship (29-49).

The Distinction between Declaration and Realization

The distinction between declaration and realization of church fellowship is important for a better understanding of the Agreement. Certainly the aim of the text's authors is not to stress this distinction and to separate two inseparable facts. Their concern, in fact, is to guarantee that church fellowship be effectively established and not limited to the signing of a theological statement. Ecumenical agreements among churches run the danger of being limited to a doctrinal consensus whose translation into the life of the church is slow in coming, if not forgotten. The authors of the Leuenberg Agreement deal with the question of church fellowship in the same fashion as they treat the message of justification. Each is seen to embrace both declaration and realization.

The first stage, that of *declaring church fellowship*, is completed by assent to the agreement. In assenting, the churches agree on the understanding of the gospel as it is defined in the Agreement. They state that the condemnations in their confessions of faith have no relevance to the present state of the doctrine of the other churches assenting to the agreement. They declare themselves in full communion regarding table and pulpit fellowship, including the mutual recognition of ordinations and the possibility of intercelebration (30 to 34).

The second stage, that of *realizing* fellowship, is longer and more difficult. It is a matter of translating the declaration into the churches' lives. In ecumenical movement terminology, this process is called reception of the theological and doctrinal agreement. It is a process that points to the dynamic reality of church fellowship, a reality never set nor definitively acquired.

In the two years from 1973 to 1975, nearly seventy European churches subscribed to the Agreement and declared themselves to be in church fellowship with one another. This step was decisive, but it was only the first step. It was then a question of working out the consequences involved in realizing this church fellowship, which the Leuenberg Agreement itself defines as an effort to "strive for the fullest possible cooperation in witness and service to the world" (29).

Means of Realizing Church Fellowship

In its last section, the text of the Agreement offers four elements whose achievement should help progress along the road toward realizing church fellowship.

First comes the search for common service "rendered in love (which) turns to man in his distress and seeks to remove the causes of that distress" (36). One must recognize the common responsibility in the search for justice and peace (36).

Second, the continuation of the theological task must include ongoing doctrinal discussions. Its aim is to deepen and to firmly establish the common understanding of the gospel. Above all, one must study a certain number of doctrinal questions in which a variety of current opinions express a legitimate diversity. The diversity must remain. It is desirable, however, to verify that this diversity does not challenge the agreement on Word and sacrament so fundamental to the recently declared church fellowship (37-41).

Third, research must investigate the probable consequences of various organizational options. According to the authors and subscribers, the Agreement's task was not to work out the global consequences in matters of church law and by-laws. This task belongs to the local churches. It is for them to assess how to promote a unity that would not be detrimental to legitimate plurality and to the freedom of the minority churches. No possibility, from distant cooperation to organic union, is to be initially excluded (42-45).

Fourth, the Leuenberg Agreement must not be isolated from the general ecumenical context. The rapprochement between the Lutherans and the Reformed must bear fruit for all Lutheran and Reformed churches worldwide. This new impetus can in turn be used for other dialogues with churches of other confessions.

In order for these four elements not to become a dead letter or remain pious wishes, the constituting assembly of Leuenberg (1973) added two organizational instruments that are not mentioned in the Agreement but whose activity has been decisive over the first fifteen years. The first of these instruments is the convening of regular plenary assemblies of the churches subscribing to the Agreement. These assemblies assess progress to date and propose new directions. They receive interim results and pass them on to churches. The first assembly met in Sigtuna (Sweden) in June of 1976,[2] the second in Driebergen (the Netherlands) in February of 1981,[3] the third in Strasbourg (France) in March of 1987.[4] A fourth is anticipated for the year 1993. The second organizational instrument is the setting up of a continuation committee (now called the executive committee), composed of about ten members representing the various churches. This committee coordinates research carried out between plenary assemblies. It normally meets twice a year and is co-chaired by a Lutheran and a Reformed. A theologian working full time or part time runs its secretariat.

This rather skeletal structure has functioned now for fifteen years, long enough to draw some conclusions. On the one hand, two of the four elements suggested by the Agreement have generated minimal concrete results. The search for a common commitment in the face of ethical, social, and political challenges (*Witness and Service*, LA 36) and the possible establishment of common structures at the level of the national or regional church have hardly given rise to any noteworthy developments. On the other hand, the other two elements, namely the continuation of theological dialogue and the attempt to understand Leuenberg in a more general ecumenical context, have been at the center of research over the years. And so I come to my second topic.

THE CONTINUATION OF THEOLOGICAL DIALOGUE

From the very beginning, the model suggested by the Agreement created a certain amount of discussion. The authors adopted the perspective on unity found in Article 7 of the Augsburg Confession, which distinguishes between the necessary agreement on the gospel and the legitimate diversity of human traditions, rites, and ceremonies. Some disagreed with this perspective, saying that "human traditions" also seemed to include different theological opinions or schools, for example on matters of ministries, baptismal practice, the two kingdom doctrine, and the doctrine of the sovereignty of Jesus Christ. Could it be that the Leuenberg Agreement settled for a "minimal consensus"? Did it pay too little attention to different and diverging theological strands and consolidate them too readily as "human traditions"? In reality, did these strands deal with subjects on which a consensus is required? The authors of the Agreement tried to show that the common understanding of justification as the message of the free grace of God (6-16) is much more than an understanding of a single doctrine. It includes a consensus on God, Jesus Christ, the Holy Spirit, the church, the sacraments, the new obedience, and so forth. If such is the case and if Leuenberg offers not a minimal consensus but the widest possible communion, it is imperative that this communion become visible through a real convergence on less primary but yet significant theological questions.

Conscious of what was at stake and anxious to show that the Agreement was not a minimal consensus, the subscribing churches committed themselves to continuing the dialogue on a certain number of questions: hermeneutical questions concerning the understanding of Scripture, the confession of faith and the church; the relation between law and gospel, baptismal practice, ministry and ordination, the two kingdom doctrine and the doctrine of the sovereignty of Christ, and church and society (39).

Work on these questions began with the assembly in Sigtuna in 1976. The organizational structure focused on "regional groups": a subscribing church organized a dialogue over several years and invited to it representatives of some fifteen other churches from throughout Europe. The results of these studies were to be assessed and, if possible, approved and adopted at the next plenary assembly.

The Two Kingdom Doctrine and the Doctrine of the Sovereignty of Jesus Christ

Initiated in 1976 at Sigtuna,[5] the final report on this dialogue was presented and approved by the Driebergen assembly in 1981.[6] The adopted document clarifies the link between these two concepts, namely the two kingdom doctrine and the doctrine of the sovereignty of Christ. These two concepts are not identical. One characterizes the Lutheran tradition, the other one the Reformed tradition. They have undergone numerous modifications in the course of these churches' histories. Yet, in their basis and intent they must be considered complementary. Both have their starting point in faith in the prevenient and justifying grace given by God through the cross and resurrection of Jesus Christ. In his love, God does not abandon the world but includes it in the divine will. The justification of the sinner encompasses a true change in his or her life and a commitment to work for a world in closer conformity to God's will.

Each in its own way, the two doctrines express this fundamental conviction of the Reformation. The Lutheran concept underscores that citizenship in the kingdom of God frees one for a commitment in the present world. Its danger lies in a false understanding which could favor quietism and a disinterest in the world's affairs. The Reformed concept underscores that the Lordship of Jesus Christ applies to all facets of life. Its danger lies in confusing the kingdom of God with a progressive transformation of the world. The Driebergen assembly acknowledged that both understandings are certainly different in their approach to resolving the question of the political and social commitment of Christians and of the churches. Thus, this difference is both complementary and stimulating. It does not "justify a separation between Churches,"[7] for it is borne by a fundamental consensus.

Ministry, Ministries, Services, and Ordination

This task had also been entrusted to regional groups at the Sigtuna assembly.[8] Preliminary results were received by the Driebergen assembly, which asked for further study.[9] This study was only completed in 1987 for the Strasbourg assembly[10] and was then approved by it. The results of the study are presented as two sets of theses: those of Neuendettelsau (1986), which the plenary assembly adopted, and those of Tampere (1986), which the assembly acknowledged. Consequently, the first set has a different status from the second. Several points, which are theologically essential, are brought forth:

First, God gives the church several ministries and services to ensure that it can fulfill its mission. The practical organization of these ministries and services varies among individual churches.

Second, a very special place belongs to the ministry of the preaching of the Word and the celebration of the sacraments (*Neuendettelsau* I 3 C). This specific ministry is instituted by God and given to the church. It is not above the church but is a service within

41

it. The ministry of the proclamation of the Word and the administration of the sacraments does not derive from the local community. It is placed over against it while at the same time being inseparable from the priesthood of all believers, a priesthood which these believers live in their prayers, in their witness, and in their service (I 3 C).

Third, the ministry is instituted by the Word of God and not vice-versa. It is at the service of the word and of the faith, at the service of the justification of the sinner and not of the justification of the Church and its organization. It is integrated into the apostolicity of the whole church (I 3 C).

Fourth, the churches born of the Reformation affirm the necessity of the *episkope*, which assumes different structures depending on the church. The Church is not based on the episcopal ministry, but the latter is given to it as a ministry of unity (I 3 D).

Fifth, through baptism, any Christian is capable of celebrating the word and sacraments. Within the church, however, this activity is entrusted to certain persons who have received a specific call and are ordained to this ministry. Ordination is both a "capacity" entrusted by God and a mission entrusted by the Church to proclaim the word and to celebrate the sacraments. Ordination happens through the laying on of hands and *epiclesis* (Neuendettelsau II 4). It is celebrated during the worship service (II 6) and is totally removed from any considerations of race or gender (II 5). Its validity extends throughout one's life (II 7). It must be distinguished from an act of installation in any particular place (II 9). All who preach the word and celebrate the sacraments must be ordained to this specific ministry (II 9).

The so-called Neuendettelsau theses, adopted in Strasbourg in the plenary assembly, point to a significant rapprochement concerning the ministry. They explain why, in light of preliminary studies, the Driebergen assembly was able to state as early as 1981 that the remaining differences in the understanding of the ministry were not church dividing.[11] The Tampere theses, received by the Strasbourg assembly, describe the situation in which the Lutheran and Reformed churches in Europe live. These theses must be perceived as a commentary explaining the Neuendettelsau theses, the latter carrying authority.

Baptismal Practice

The Leuenberg Agreement acknowledges the basic consensus existing between Lutherans and Reformed in Europe regarding baptism: "In baptism, Jesus Christ irrevocably receives man, fallen prey to sin and death, into his fellowship of salvation so that he may become a new creature. In the power of his Holy Spirit, he calls him into his community and to a new life of faith, to daily repentance, and to discipleship" (LA 14). This same Agreement decides, however, to put the question of "baptismal practice" on the agenda of future dialogues (39). This step is prompted by certain reservations on the part of some churches from Southern Europe which, as tiny minority communities, often share a common understanding with "Baptist-type" churches, also in the minority. While subscribing to the common definition of baptism, they express reservations at the practical level about a view of baptism that would be too "magical" and about a perceived lack of emphasis placed on the faith of the baptized.

Other churches were concerned about the baptismal practices of these Southern European churches. Thus, in spite of the consensus already reached, baptismal theology and practice required further reflection. This decision was reached in 1981 by the Driebergen assembly, which initiated a regional dialogue on this question.[12] The results were presented in Strasbourg.[13] They are organized into four chapters offering a remarkably elaborate theology of baptism, which was approved by nearly all of the churches represented. Nevertheless, they could not be adopted. Some Southern European churches (in particular the Waldensian Church of Italy) expressed reservations, especially about the necessity of baptism to salvation. Adoption of this text was postponed until the following assembly, and the intervening time set aside for theological reflection and dialogue with the churches who expressed reservations.[14]

Our intention is not to enumerate here these various theses on baptism, which would probably be acceptable to other Christian traditions. We mentioned this ongoing dialogue in order to show the pressing *need* for dialogues following the signing of the Agreement itself. Each group places a different emphasis on this non-unanimity concerning certain aspects of baptism. Some consider that the very foundation of the Agreement is jeopardized; others find it to be a mere episode of no major consequence. Church fellowship is indeed declared through the signing of the Agreement. This declaration calls for implementation, which in turn leads to reassessing the scope of the declared consensus, as in this example of baptism. Theological dialogue continues to pursue this goal and is nowadays an indispensable tool of the communion born in Leuenberg.

Many of the themes listed in article 39 of the Leuenberg Agreement have not been sufficiently studied to allow for the drafting of an agreement (for example, the unfinished study on law and gospel). Other themes have not yet been placed on the agenda. The Strasbourg assembly set as new priorities dialogues on ecclesiology (the understanding of the Church) and on Christian witness as it relates to freedom. This new stage has just begun, and dialogue groups have barely started their work.

THE GENERAL ECUMENICAL CONTEXT

The Agreement's second dimension, on which the subscribing churches have specifically concentrated, is the promotion of "the ecumenical fellowship of all Christian churches" (LA 46). Different from theological dialogues, this effort does not necessarily lead to the drafting of texts. It is therefore more difficult to judge its impact and its breadth. It is obvious to the churches subscribing to the Agreement, however, that their special fellowship is but one element, even if it is decisive and original, within the general ecumenical context. Many positions taken in confessions and texts from general assemblies testify to this fact. The Strasbourg assembly even adopted it as its key subject. Doctrinal dialogues have, whenever possible, taken into account the dialogues among other traditions. Multiple contacts and the participation in the assemblies of observers from other churches are small additional signs. Two elements are, however, particularly important and must be mentioned in connection with this concern to define the churches of the Leuenberg Agreement within the more general ecumenical context.

Reflection upon Baptism, Eucharist, and Ministry

The churches subscribing to the Agreement are all individual members of the World Council of Churches. Thus they responded separately to *Baptism, Eucharist, and Ministry,* the "Lima document," issued by Faith and Order. We must, however, note that between 1981 and 1984 the Berlin dialogue group tried to formulate a certain number of criteria for stands taken on *BEM,* criteria which could be common to the Lutheran and Reformed churches of Europe.[15] Since each church has taken a stand for itself, the aim was not to define the elements of a potential common position. Rather, it was to understand each of the three chapters of *BEM* as closely linked to the theological strands of the Leuenberg Agreement. The aim was also to note at the same time the questions that the Reformation churches must put to *BEM* and the challenges that the document addresses to the subscribers of Leuenberg. It is difficult to judge the impact and the general breadth of these criteria within the subscribing churches. It seems to have been less in the large churches. From the Strasbourg assembly, we have learned that these criteria were very useful to the small minority churches in helping them to understand more clearly what was at stake in the text from Faith and Order.

Reflection on the Identity of the Churches Born of the Reformation

In conjunction with reflection on the Lima document, the churches subscribing to Leuenberg decided to specify the particular contributions to the modern ecumenical movement of the traditions from the sixteenth-century Reformation. In regard to this activity, which was decided by the Driebergen assembly,[16] the coordinating committee appealed to ecumenical institutes for help. A memorandum, "The Churches Born of the Reformation and the Ecumenical Movement," was drafted in 1984.[17] This text recalls the basic theological strands of the Reformation: justification by faith, Word of God, Scripture and tradition, church and ministry, as well as the act of confessing and the confession of faith and especially the links between these various elements that might bear fruit for the whole of the ecumenical movement. The text also strives to delineate some broader ecumenical activities in which the churches born of the Reformation could participate.

At that level, it appears that the directions recommended by the representatives of each church are not identical. Some stress the common heritage that encompasses, beyond the Lutherans and the Reformed, the "left wing" of the Reformation, the Baptist churches and others. They would broaden the Agreement to include these traditions and would not be totally opposed to the idea of a "block of reforming churches." This group could then defend *together* the heritage of the Reformation within the ecumenical movement. It could enter into dialogues with the Catholic and Orthodox churches and thus put an end to separate Reformed and Lutheran dialogues with these traditions. According to the defenders of this thesis, these separate dialogues are the reason for a progressive estrangement between the Lutherans and the Reformed of Europe, a divergence that implicitly questions Leuenberg.

The other thesis, which is no less strongly defended—especially by Lutheran representatives—insists that Leuenberg cannot serve as a basis for the creation of a "reforming block." Leuenberg is a bilateral agreement limited to Lutherans and Reformed. There is no reason to feel closer to Baptist churches than to the Roman Catholic church, since at present full church fellowship has been realized with neither of these two traditions. The supporters of this thesis have striven to show that their bilateral dialogues, in particular with Rome and Canterbury, demonstrate a perfect loyalty to the Lutheran-Reformed fellowship. According to them, there is no case where a rapprochement with these traditions would question the achievements of the Leuenberg Agreement.

Representatives of both trends met to formulate together the basic convictions of the churches born of the Reformation and to strive for a true deepening of the church fellowship resulting from the Leuenberg Agreement. They could agree that the thinking linked to this memorandum intends in no way to "disassociate the churches born of the Reformation from the ecumenical movement." This memorandum is not to be used to "oppose the tradition of our churches to that of the other churches, through the defining of specific values. It is rather the common striving for unity which makes this self-reflection necessary and which must be understood, to a certain extent, as a 'pre-conciliar process' leading to the conciliar fellowship of all the churches." [18]

The case of this memorandum brings to light the difficulty of reaching a common global ecumenical perspective inside the community of the churches subscribing to the Leuenberg Agreement. Nor is the debate unique to Leuenberg. A parallel can be drawn with debates that have existed or do exist at the level of the World Council of Churches, or in the confessional families themselves. Within the group of subscribers to Leuenberg, it translates into different ways of understanding the intent and the scope of the Agreement. While stressing the independence of each subscribing church, some wish it to be a charter of European Protestantism. Others consider it to be the text of a bilateral agreement which has the same scope and the same authority as other similar texts. Of course there is a whole range of positions in between.

The drafting of this memorandum has also brought out the pressing necessity of reflecting upon the *compatibility* of dialogues. Certain churches subscribing to Leuenberg are in communion with the Methodist churches (Federal Republic of Germany, Italy); others are not. Some feel close to the Baptists (Italy, Spain), others to the Catholics. The Lutherans are preparing to enter into church fellowship with the Anglicans. We could give countless examples. The question of compatibility is asked. Do my friends include the friends of my friends? The churches subscribing to the Agreement have become aware of that problem. G. Gassmann's paper at the Strasbourg assembly dealt with this issue. That same assembly charged its executive committee to study the question carefully. [19]

EVALUATION AND PERSPECTIVES

Evaluation

It is impossible to judge in a few words the consequences of the Leuenberg Agreement. Global appraisal would be too general.

The very presentation of facts shows the coexistence of positive aspects with elements evoking some reservations.

Concerning the latter, the criticism most often heard states that the Agreement has not brought about any change in church life. The great challenges of society are not taken up; interest seems to center on certain nonurgent theological questions. At the level of local church life, the Agreement only ratified a state of affairs without generating a real rapprochement between Reformed and Lutheran communities. These criticisms indirectly touch on the two areas stated in the Agreement as places for the realization of fellowship: the search for a common witness and service and the consequences of the Agreement on the organizational level. Neither of these concerns has been truly central in the past.

This criticism must not be taken lightly. It is correct and well-founded. The churches subscribing to the Agreement must make a genuine effort in these two areas. The realization of church fellowship is still not satisfactory. In too many instances, the Agreement serves as a pretext for cementing the status quo. Moreover, the Agreement's function often varies widely according to the region. In Germany, for instance, the Agreement serves to manage the relationship among the regional churches, which are Lutheran, Reformed, or Union. In most cases, within an area, there is one single regional church. In other countries, like Hungary, France and the Netherlands, Lutherans and Reformed live in the same area as two churches with separate structures. In these last countries mentioned, progress seems most difficult to obtain. At times, one may wonder if the Leuenberg Agreement has gone beyond being a mere theological text signed some fifteen years ago.

On the positive side, one must not forget that the model of unity offered by the Agreement is one of the only models of church fellowship that has reached the stage of any concrete implementation. The very existence of this model and of this fellowship has significant ecclesiological impact for all Christian churches on their path toward unity. Moreover, there are numerous signs indicating a slow but real change in the Lutheran-Reformed relationship in Europe. These signs include the opportunity for a pastor from one church to minister to a community of another tradition, and the fact that Lutherans can participate in the church life of the Reformed (or vice-versa) when they arrive in an area where their tradition is not represented. There are many others. During their synods, the individual churches have learned to take into account the Agreement and wider church fellowship. We can cite the example of the Reformed Church of France, which corrected, at the request of the coordinating committee, some of its surprising decisions concerning ordination. Many other examples could be mentioned, including the drawing from the heritage of another tradition in writing new hymn books. In a more global way, we must stress the post-Leuenberg theological work which we have mentioned, be it research on specific points (for instance the ministry) or the attempt at understanding Leuenberg in a more general ecumenical context.

Scholarly analysis and dialogue uncover a multifaceted but somewhat predictable and even controllable body of material with its strengths and weaknesses. The main difficulty encountered in church fellowship goes beyond this to the difficulty known to all dialogue groups: that is, the stage of *reception* at all levels of church life, particularly at the local level. Leuenberg has known the difficulties of the reception process now for nearly fifteen years. In this context, certain questions without satisfactory solutions reappear periodically. How are we to motivate local communities that do not want things to change? How are we to surmount the nondoctrinal, ethical, cultural, economic and linguistic factors that, in many places, distinguish Lutherans from Reformed? Is the institutional tool that these churches have given themselves insufficient? Above all, how are we to understand the authority of a text adopted by a plenary assembly (for instance the theses on ministry which were approved in Strasbourg in 1987) and to press the individual churches that participated in its drafting to acknowledge its authoritative character?

Perspectives

In the spring of 1987, the Strasbourg assembly tried to assess the situation and to lay out future directions. Concerning the local situation, it could only invite the individual churches to translate into their daily lives the results that have already been obtained. The coordinating committee, composed mainly of theologians in charge of dialogues, has become an executive committee with a wider representation of church leaders. This new committee now has the mandate to monitor the whole process of realizing church fellowship. It will call on ecumenical institutes for tasks of a more specific theological nature.[20]

This committee has received the following mandate:

- to pursue theological dialogues on the subjects mentioned in paragraph 39 of the Agreement. The themes chosen for the coming years are ecclesiology (with, as background, the whole problematic mentioned in the "identity of the reforming churches") and the Christian understanding of freedom (its link with justification by faith and the commitment of Christians in society);[21]

- to set up immediately a common witness and service of the Lutheran and Reformed churches in Europe in light of the major challenges of our times. Hence, it has been decided that the churches subscribing to Leuenberg will participate actively in the preparation and realization of the convocation "Justice, Peace and Integrity of Creation" first on a European level in Basel in 1989, then on a global level in 1990;[22]

- to monitor closely the Lutheran–Reformed church fellowship born in Europe so that it fits into the more general ecumenical context. Hence the collaboration with Faith and Order on the Lima document and its consequences will continue, and special attention will focus on the question raised about the compatibility of ecumenical dialogues.[23]

These directions were worked out last year. The executive committee has just adopted the first measures which will make the implementation possible. It is of course too early to judge in any way these new mandates that take up paths suggested by preceding assemblies, but with new and original emphases.

Notes

1. "Theses on Church Fellowship. Preparatory Discussions to Leuenberg," E. Schieffer, *Von Schauenberg nach Leuenberg*. *Entstehung und Bedeutung der Konkordie reformatorischer Kirchen in Europe*. (Bonifatius Paderborn, 1983), Theses of 1970, A63. See also M. Lienhard, *Lutherish-reformierte Kirchengemeinschaft heute*, 2nd ed. ökumenische Perspektiven 2 (Frankfurt, 1973).

2. The Sigtuna Report: *Zeugnis und Dienst reformatorischer Kirchen im Europa der Gegenwart*, ed. M. Lienhard. ökumenische Perspektiven 8, (Frankfurt, 1977). (Hereafter cited as "Sigtuna Report.")

3. The Driebergen Report: *Konkordie und Kirchengemeinschaft reformatorischer Kirchen im Europa der Gegenwart*, ed. A. Birmelé. ökumenische Perspektiven 10 (Frankfurt, 1982). (Hereafter cited as "Driebergen Report.")

4. The Strasbourg Report: *Konkordie und ökumene. Die Leuenberger Kirchengemeinschaft in der gegenwärtigen ökumenischen Situation*, ed. A. Birmelé (Frankfurt, 1988). (Hereafter cited as "Strasbourg Report.")

5. "Sigtuna Report," 154, see also lectures of J. Hempel and A. Dumas, 39-76.

6. "Driebergen Report," 2.2, 109. See the reports of the "Berlin" and "Amsterdam" groups, 39-51 and the discussion which took place in Driebergen, 115-117.

7. *Ibid.*, 115.

8. Sigtuna Report, 154, see the preparatory studies of G. Gassmann and D. von Allmen, 77-144.

9. "Driebergen Report," 109. See the reports of the "Copenhagen" and "South-East Europe" groups, 52-76, and the discussion which took place in Driebergen, 118.

10. "Strasbourg Report," 146; "Copenhagen" group report, 61-77.

11. "Driebergen Report," 2.3, 110.

12. *Ibid.*, 113, 5.3.

13. "Strasbourg Report," 51-61.

14. *Ibid.*, 146.

15. *Ibid.*, 15-37.

16. "Driebergen Report" 4.2, 111.

17. French text of the Memorandum in *Foi et Vie* 85 (1986): 3-54. German text in *EPD Dokumentation* 49a, November 1984.

18. Memorandum, paragraph 6.

19. "Strasbourg Report" Decision 7, 151.

20. "Strasbourg Report" Decision 5, 3.2 and 5.1, 148.

21. "Strasbourg Report" Decision 6, 149.

22. "Strasbourg Report" Decision 4, 147.

23. See the "Strasbourg Report" Decision 6 and 7, 150.

4

Critique of the Leuenberg Agreement as an Ecumenical Model

THE BACKGROUND

From Dialogue to Fellowship

The 1973 Leuenberg Agreement grew out of a daily lived fellowship between Reformed and Lutheran Christians and communities. Theologically and historically speaking, however, it arose, as we have seen, out of the preceding Lutheran–Reformed doctrinal conversations both on national and European levels, and out of the consensus these conversations had achieved with regard to controversial church-dividing issues.

After the consensus had been achieved, the question that arose comes up more and more often in our various dialogues and that indeed, should be asked after every successful ecumenical dialogue: What now? Where do things go from here? This question *must* be asked, otherwise dialogue has deteriorated into a kind of theological game, into an ecumenical "art for art's sake," and has forgotten its goal: the realization of unity. That unity does not arise automatically out of an achieved theological consensus; the attractive biblical parable of the growing seed does not apply here: "A man should scatter seed upon the ground, and should sleep and rise night and day, and the seed should sprout and grow, he knows not how" (Mark 4:27).

On the contrary, a new and deliberate effort is required in order to transform theological consensus into lived church fellowship. Today we refer to this effort, which stretches from the establishment of consensus in the dialogue to the realization of fellowship between the churches as "ecumenical reception," a term which then, at the end of the sixties, was almost unused, even unknown. At the same time it became plain that a clear idea of what church fellowship or church unity is, of what this fellowship looks like and of how it must be structured, represents an indispensable aid in this effort of transforming theological consensus into a lived church fellowship.

Consequently, the theme of the next round of European Lutheran–Reformed conversations was "Church Fellowship and Church Division." And it was only logical that at the same time two changes were made vis à vis the Bad Schauenburg dialogues: first of all, for the sake of a stronger involvement of the churches themselves, it was no longer only professional theologians who took part in the dialogue, but also church leaders and pastors; second, it was no longer only the Department for Faith and Order of the WCC which planned and was responsible for the dialogue, but also the two World Federations—the World Alliance of Reformed Churches and the Lutheran World Federation. (I myself happened to be the responsible secretary for the LWF.)

Rejected Concepts of Unity

The question asked at the two Leuenberg meetings (1969 and 1970) was "What concept of church unity or church fellowship should be set forth as the objective and what are the requirements for the realization of this objective?

The ecumenical context offered *two* already tested concepts or models of unity that could have been applied. One of the models was that of the German "United Churches," the model of the Old Prussian Union as it had found its application in various forms during the course of the first half of the 19th century. A good percentage of the participants in the Lutheran–Reformed dialogues, indeed, came from such "United Churches." For the most part these are churches where the existing Lutheran and Reformed confessions (on the Lutheran side primarily the *Confessio Augustana* and Luther's *Small Catechism*, on the Reformed side the *Heidelberg Catechism*), remain valid and operative and where, on account of this, there are confessionally different congregations. However, on the basis of the common confession of Jesus Christ as the only Lord, of the Holy Scripture as the only source and norm, and of the ancient creeds, this confessional difference was declared officially to be unessential[1] and therefore no longer divisive, even though, for this judgment, there are no binding theological grounds in the form of officially and mutually accepted consensus statements.

The second model that could have been applied at Leuenberg was the model of church union as it was realized for the first time in the United Church of Canada (1925) and toward which church union negotiations particularly in Asia and Africa—but here too in the U.S. (COCU)—are striving. This concept of unity has been called "organic" or "corporative union." Its fundamental characteristic is that in this union, unlike in a German United Church, all confessional identities, differences or structures are abandoned.[2] Organic or corporative union is therefore consciously *trans*-confessional, if not *anti*-confessional. It stems from the fusion of the existing confessional traditions and identities and gives rise to a new church with a new name and a new identity. This organic union was considered in the Faith and Order Movement and then also in the WCC, at least up until New Delhi (1961), to be the ideal, the true form of visible (local) church unity.

At the beginning of the Leuenberg conversations both these concepts or models of unity were possible options. However, as far as I can remember, the first model, i.e. the model of the German United Churches, was never seriously discussed at Leuenberg. That may seem surprising, but is not really. For all previous conversations between Reformed and Lutherans, which in Germany always involved United Church participants, had aimed at overcoming the

United Churches' shortcoming, i.e. the absence of an official theological consensus that would show and explain *why* the confessional differences between Lutherans and Reformed are not or no longer church-dividing. Thus, the first model had implicitly been left behind already, and therefore played hardly any further role in the Leuenberg conversations.

But what about the second model, that of the trans-confessional organic union. I remember a short but very heated debate in which two participants advocated this model as the only true and worthwhile goal. But the rejection by the vast majority was equally emphatic. The idea of a union in the sense of a trans-confessional merger of churches never stood a chance at Leuenberg, either from a Lutheran or Reformed point of view.

And so it was clear: Leuenberg had—and that was to prove important for the whole of ecumenism—to develop something along the lines of an independent and in many respects new concept of unity.

Three Principles of Ecumenism

I have spoken of a concept of unity which in many respects was new. In fact, at Leuenberg there was no need to start right from scratch. For, since the Second World War and primarily in Germany in connection with the restructuring of the German churches (the founding of the Evangelical Church of Union, the Evangelical Church of Germany, and the United Evangelical Lutheran Church of Germany), but, at the same time, strongly influenced by what was happening and was being thought in the wider ecumenical movement, reflections and discussions had begun on the meaning of church, church union and church fellowship, koinonia, pulpit and altar fellowship, confessional fellowship, etc.

What happened was twofold: First, the notion of "church fellowship" (*Kirchengemeinschaft*), which for the time being was used very generally and unspecifically, moved more and more to the center of attention and thereby began to develop into a specific concept of unity. Secondly, these reflections and developments were no longer confined to Germany, but were taken up and developed in the Lutheran World Federation, particularly in the LWF's theological commission—and thereby on an international level.

I will spare myself and my audience the details of this development.[3] What is important is to explain the content of this concept of "church fellowship," conversations of 1969-70 and then in its application by the "Leuenberg Agreement" of 1973. However, before I elucidate this specific concept of church fellowship in a few points, we should recall three principles that are valid for every form and for every concept of authentic church unity and that as such are approved by all churches engaged in the current ecumenical movement:

- First principle: We cannot *make* Christian unity or fellowship (koinonia) through agreements, consensus, accords, or unification. Christian unity or fellowship is first and foremost God-given fellowship with Christ himself: We belong to his Body by faith in his Word and by the receiving of baptism and the Eucharist. Since Christians live in this fellowship with Christ himself, they also live in fellowship with each other.

- Second principle: Even if we cannot make Christian unity or fellowship, we are, nevertheless, instructed to *live* this God-given fellowship, to make it visible and noticeable for us and for others, and to protect and to maintain it: in the fellowship of faith and proclamation, in the fellowship of the sacraments, in the fellowship of ministry, and in common church life, common witness, and common service to the world.

- Third principle: Our ecumenical task and our ecumenical endeavor for fellowship are not directed toward uniformity. In Christ's Church there is a legitimate and necessary diversity of gifts and services, of expressions of faith and confession, of forms of piety and witness, of structures for life and service, which must not be repressed.

All concepts and models of authentic church unity fit into this comprehensive framework, even if, on the basis of the specific characteristics, they differ from each other and seem, in many respects, even to exist in tension with each other.

The concept of church fellowship as taken up and developed by the Leuenberg conversations, and as applied by the "Leuenberg Agreement," also fits within the framework of the three above-mentioned principles.

CHURCH FELLOWSHIP ACCORDING TO THE LEUENBERG AGREEMENT

So, what is this "church fellowship" according to the Leuenberg Agreement?

Here we can refer to the whole of Section 4 of the Agreement (29-49), dealing with "The Declaration and Realization of Church Fellowship." Particularly important are the following points:

> "In the sense intended in this Agreement, church fellowship means that, on the basis of the consensus they have reached in their understanding of the gospel, churches with different confessional positions accord each other fellowship in word and sacrament, and strive for the fullest possible cooperation in witness and service to the world" (29).
>
> "This includes the mutual recognition of ordination and the freedom to provide for intercelebration" (33).
>
> "The doctrinal condemnations expressed in the confessional documents no longer apply to the contemporary doctrinal position of the assenting churches" (32).

On the basis of these statements and in light of the discussions and reflections behind them, it is possible to elucidate in five points what church fellowship is according to the Leuenberg Agreement. I will sum up each of these five points in the form of a thesis and comment on it as briefly as possible.

First, church fellowship is a full realization of the unity of the church. It comprises all essential elements of church unity: fellowship in faith, fellowship in the sacraments, fellowship in ministry, fellowship in church life and in witness and service to the world, (29 and 33).

The "second principle" mentions these four constitutive elements of Church unity. It takes up what had been said in the great ecumenical statements on the unity of the Church, for example in the famous New Delhi Formula of the WCC (1961), in the LWF's Budapest statement, *The Unity We Seek* (1984), and even in the *Decree of Ecumenism* of the Second Vatican Council (1964). Thereby the concept of church fellowship is on one and the same level with all other concepts or models of unity which integrate these four basic elements of church unity and which as a result can claim to realize full church unity.

Consequently, church fellowship according to the Leuenberg Agreement is not merely to be understood as a preliminary or intermediary stage on the way toward church unity, as has on occasion been maintained. It is to be understood as a form of full church unity, as—to use the Anglo-Saxon term—*full communion*. However, the Leuenberg Agreement refers at the same time to specific features that characterize the concept of church fellowship and make it differ from other concepts of unity.

And so the second point: church fellowship is fellowship between "churches with different confessional positions" (29).

Here lies a basic ruling (*Grundentscheidung*) of the Leuenberg conversations that is important for the whole ecumenical movement: It implies that the variety and diversity among confessional traditions and identities are not *as such* church dividing. A given confessional heritage can, indeed, belong within the realm of legitimate and even necessary variety and not need to be abandoned for the sake of unity. The above-mentioned and universally recognized "third principle," that the unity of the Church embraces diversity and does not mean uniformity, is therefore applied to the phenomenon of confessional diversity. The ecumenical path following from this is therefore no longer that of a "*unification* of churches" but that of "*mutual recognition*."

Here the Leuenberg Agreement takes up a train of ecumenical thought that at the beginning of the ecumenical movement was approved by many—not least of all by representatives of the Lutheran churches—but that later receded almost completely into the background.[4]

Third, church fellowship between confessionally different churches becomes possible by means of a binding doctrinal consensus with regard to what is fundamental or central to the understanding of the gospel and to its proclamation in word and sacrament ("basic consensus").

The first of the constitutive elements for church unity or church fellowship is, as we saw, fellowship in faith. If, however, it is true that church unity or church fellowship does not mean uniformity, but unity or fellowship in diversity, the "third principle," then, likewise, fellowship in faith does not mean uniformity but unity and diversity at one and the same time. There can therefore be fellowship in faith without our thinking and talking exactly alike in *all* aspects of faith and confession.

Does this betray the requirement that a consensus in faith and doctrine must exist between churches desiring fellowship with each other? Not in the slightest! That would only be the case if one were to understand this consensus as a total agreement of all points, aspects, and terminology of faith and doctrine. But that is not the belief of the Reformation. Article 7 of the *Confessio Augustana* played a decisive role here in defining the concept of church fellowship, particularly with the distinction it makes between that which is *"enough* for true unity of the Church" *(satis est)* and that which *"is not necessary (nec necesse est).*[5] The idea of church fellowship between churches of different confessional positions is thus only meaningful if one succeeds in distinguishing between what is "fundamental" and necessary for unity on the one hand, and what is "secondary" and not necessary for church unity on the other hand.[6] It was only because this distinction was able to succeed in the Leuenberg conversations that the Leuenberg Agreement and the realization of church fellowship between the confessionally different Lutheran and Reformed churches could also succeed.

Today we would say that the concept of church fellowship stands or falls with the idea that what is necessary and *sufficient* for the unity of the Church is a *basic* consensus—not a *full* consensus. According to the Leuenberg Agreement what is fundamental for the unity of the Church is "the true understanding of the gospel . . .

expressed . . . in the doctrine of justification'' (8) and the ensuing conception of word and sacrament (10-16).

Fourth, for the establishment of church fellowship the invalidation of previous mutual doctrinal condemnations is required (32). Such an invalidation confirms that the achieved basic consensus is indeed enough for the unity of the church and that divisive differences no longer exist.

Here too the Leuenberg conversations and the Leuenberg Agreement have accomplished pioneering work. Wherever the "third principle''—i.e. the conviction that unity does not mean uniformity, but can and must embrace diversity—is taken seriously and applied it must be shown how, in light of the achieved basic consensus, the diversity that up to now has existed, and which to some extent still exists, is no longer church-dividing. This is particularly necessary where the doctrinal differences between the churches were handled by "mutual condemnations," as happened in the confessional writings of the Reformation.

So, if church fellowship is a fellowship between churches in which the existing confessions remain valid and operative, it must be shown and declared by an official pronouncement that those doctrinal condemnations are no longer relevant to the partner churches. If this cannot be done, the consensus which has been reached is not yet that *basic* consensus which is enough for the unity of the church.

The whole of Section 3 (17-28) of the "Leuenberg Agreement" is devoted to this invalidation of previous mutual doctrinal condemnations.

Fifth, once established ("declared"), church fellowship demands to be "realized," to the greatest possible extent, in all areas of church life and practice, i.e. to be lived, maintained, strengthened, consolidated and thereby protected from lifelessness, atrophy and superficiality.

Most people at Leuenberg were aware that in Protestantism—not least of all in Lutheranism!—there is a traditional, deep-seated tendency to confine the unity of the church to a primarily spiritual fellowship. Very often it was only with aversion that unity of the church was thought also to signify fellowship in everyday life and practice of the church—a fellowship which is simply inconceivable without a certain amount of common structure and organization. So, for the most part, church fellowship was confined to fellowship in faith ("confessional fellowship") and to the "pulpit and altar fellowship" that this made possible.

During the Leuenberg conversations, however, it became evident that where these points were concerned, the insights and experiences of the wider ecumenical movement had not been without effect. Certainly the concept of "organic unity," which heavily emphasizes the organizational aspects of church unity, was rejected. But it was sensed that this concept, with its stress on common church life and practice, common constitution and structure, did contain an element of truth, which must be included in church fellowship.

However, those at Leuenberg felt that they could not lay down detailed guidelines as to how this common structuring of church life and practice was to come about and how it was to look in a future Lutheran–Reformed church fellowship in different European countries and settings. So the outcome went no further than to assert, very firmly, that a "declaration" of church fellowship (30-34) was not sufficient, but that this church fellowship, by its very nature, must be "realized," i.e. be "lived" (35-49: esp. 35). The established or declared church fellowship, so it read in the 1970 Leuenberg Report, "impels" by its very essence "the greatest possible fellowship in inner church life and in witness and service to the world."[7]

This impetus toward realization, the deepening and strengthening of fellowship in church life and practice, in "witness and service" (36), in the "continuing theological task" (37-41), with regard to "organizational consequences" and "unification" and in the ecumenical field (46-49) is an integral part of church fellowship according to the Leuenberg Agreement. The concept of church fellowship must not be envisaged without this impetus.

So much for the description of church fellowship according to the Leuenberg Agreement. I want now to try in one paragraph to sum up what has been said: Church fellowship is a full realization of church unity. It is fellowship in faith, in the sacraments, in ministry, and in life and work between confessionally different churches. It is borne by a "basic consensus" on the understanding of the gospel and its transmission in word and sacrament, in light of which the previous mutual doctrinal condemnations cease to apply to today's partners.

QUESTIONS ADDRESSED TO LEUENBERG

The Leuenberg conversations and the Agreement emanating from them were of course closely related to a definite historical and ecumenical setting. In this setting the concept of church fellowship, as it then began to take shape, had in many respects a pioneering role in ecumenism. It had an effect on the discussions in the 1970s of concepts of unity and models of unification, and it was godfather to the concept of "unity in reconciled diversity," which at that time stepped aside for the concept of "conciliar fellowship" and was welcomed and taken over for example by the LWF in Dar es Salaam (1977).

However, ecumenical developments have continued in many respects since then. These developments have by no means dismissed the concept of church fellowship. On the contrary, they have confirmed it. Nonetheless, changes that have occurred in the ecumenical situation might now cause us to ask certain questions as to the way the concept of church fellowship was formulated at that time.

I would like to propose three such questions which can in fact be seen as impulses for further developing the concept of church fellowship.

First, would it not be appropriate to strengthen the structural element in the concept of church fellowship?

In accordance with the Leuenberg Agreement, a "fullest possible cooperation in witness and service" is an essential part of church fellowship (29) and its realization (36). However, the Agreement is very cautious when it comes to the ways and means indispensable for common decision making and common action. Such caution in the Agreement is of course justified if one takes into account the fact that the Agreement applies to many very different national or territorial churches and church situations in Europe. The question of "organizational consequences" and "organizational mergers" is therefore left up to the churches in the various countries (42-45).

However, this caution is no longer justified where the question of common practice on a European-wide basis is concerned. It is even more out of place where church fellowship is declared and realized between Lutheran and Reformed churches *within a given country*. Indeed, developments toward a strengthening of the structural element both in individual countries and on a European-wide basis very soon began to take place: In addition the "continuing doctrinal discussions" (37) provided for by the Agreement itself, we later found the establishment of an Executive Committee with its corresponding Office and regular assemblies of the churches involved in the Leuenberg Agreement. On a national level one should mention e.g. the developments in the GDR toward a closer structured fellowship between the Lutheran and United Churches.

Second, should there not be, as part of the basic consensus, a common statement in ministry?

The question of the ministry was not one of the traditionally church-dividing issues between Lutheran and Reformed churches. So it was understandable that the Lutheran–Reformed dialogues which led to the Leuenberg Agreement scarcely focused on the question of the ministry. Nonetheless the Agreement and the concept of church fellowship in no way ignore the question of the ministry: The "mutual recognition of ordination" forms a constitutive element of church fellowship (33; cf.43).

Since the question of the understanding and practice of the ministry is one of the central issues in the dialogue of the Reformation churches with the Anglican, Roman Catholic, and Orthodox churches, and since this issue is currently subject to considerable diversity as regards doctrine and practice even within the Reformation churches, it would be worth seeing whether some form of common understanding among the Reformation churches on this issue should not become part of the "basic consensus" necessary for the preservation of church fellowship. The continuing doctrinal discussions that have since taken place on "ministry and ordination" among the churches of the Leuenberg Agreement might be the way to achieve this.

How can Lutheran–Reformed church fellowship avoid being threatened or itself threatening other ecumenical developments? Since the adoption of the Leuenberg Agreement the bilateral dialogues Lutherans and Reformed with other churches have continued. There seems to be much evidence that Lutheran conversations with, for example, Anglicans and Roman Catholics have engendered agreements which the Reformed church would have difficulty in accepting; and that where the Reformed church is concerned, the conversations with, for example, Baptists and Mennonites have led to rapprochements which the Lutheran church would have difficulty in appropriating.

How can these developments be prevented from becoming a threat to Lutheran–Reformed church fellowship? And vice versa, how can one prevent Lutheran–Reformed church fellowship—in contrast to its explicit intention—from standing in the way of "the ecumenical fellowship of all Christian churches" instead of "promoting it" (46) and being "a contribution to this end" (47)?

It is very doubtful whether there is indeed any conclusive answer or ready solution to these extremely pressing issues. But everyone must do all that is ecumenically possible and let nothing remain undone. This is a basic ecumenical imperative and we must not shrink from it. Therefore, it is crucial that in church fellowship, together with our mutual commitment to the fellowship already given and our firm refusal to lose hold of each other, there is an increasing *mutual trust* in what our partner does and has to do ecumenically. In this spirit of mutual confidence and trust, we will be able to strive together to remove the threat from those emerging dissimilarities, welcoming instead the new ecumenical impulses they offer.

Notes

1. In the "Preussische Kabinettsordre" of 1817 by which the Old Prussian Union was established the term used was *ausserwesentlich*.
2. Therefore, a German "United Church" is, in ecumenical circles, not being regarded as an authentic "church union." R. Rouse/St. Ch. Neill eds., *A History of the Ecumenical*

Movement 1517–1948, 2nd edition, (London 1967), 288; cf. 454ff. See also *Öekumene-Lexikon*, 1st ed. (Frankfurt: 1983), 1192ff—particularly 1200).

3. See here my article, "Zur Enstehung und Bedeutung des Konzepts Kirchengemeinschaft," in: *Communio Sanctorum. Einheit der Christen—Einheit der Kirche. Festschrift für Bischof Paul-Werner (Würzburg:* Scheele, 1988), 204-230.

4. See my article, "Anerkennung—Ein ökumenischer Schlüsselbegriff," in *Dialog und Anerkennug.* Beiheft zur ökumenischen Rundschau No. 37 (Frankfurt, 1980), 25-41, particularly 30-34.

5. On the Reformed side, art. 17 of the *Confessio Helvetica Posterior* makes the same distinction.

6. Cf. Leuenberg Agreement which asks us, "to distinguish between the fundamental witness of the Reformation confessions of faith and their historically conditioned thought forms" (5). With particularly strong emphasis the "Leitsätze der VELKD zur Kirchengemeinschaft" of 1969 insist on this distinction (Lutherische Monatshefte 1969), 525.

7. The report on the Leuenberg conversations from 1969 to 1970—"Kirchengemeinschaft und Kirchentrennung"—can be found in: *Gemeinschaft der reformatorischen Kirchen. Auf dem Wege II* (Zürich 1971), 15; and also in Elisabeth Schieffer. *Von Schauenberg nach Leuenberg* (Paderborn, 1983), 61ff.

5

An Evaluation of the Leuenberg Agreement: A Reformed Perspective

INTRODUCTION

Remember that old vaudeville routine that entertained our forebears? The theater is pitch-black except for a large circle of light falling, as from a street lamp, front stage center. A dimly illuminated area is also visible in a far corner. In the spot of light a figure is revealed, crawling on all fours, intently searching for something. After a few moments a policeman appears. The officer sympathetically joins in the search for what he learns is a lost set of keys. After some time he asks if this is the place where the keys were lost. The man points to the dimly lit corner of the stage and says, "No, I lost them over there."

We often hunt for the missing keys of life in comfortable places, spurning those difficult spots where a key actually has been lost. Since 1962, American churches of the Lutheran and Reformed traditions have been hunting for the key to fellowship in the light of bilateral conversations that searched the 16th century to identify and neutralize church-dividing issues, wrote reports recommending unity, and in one case made bold recommendations. Now, some wonder

PAUL R. FRIES

if this is where the key to unity was lost. Should the search be moved to a new area on the ecumenical stage—perhaps into the light shed by the Leuenberg Agreement?

My task, in this quest for new light, is to explore "how from a Reformed perspective the Leuenberg Agreement is relevant to the American scene." "The American scene," of course, refers to the Lutheran and Reformed churches of this country in their quest for understanding and unity; "relevance" to that which would advance this cause. What is being asked here, then, is whether, from a Reformed view, the Leuenberg Agreement could be received by the churches of the two traditions and thus become a vehicle for the fellowship which seems so close, and yet so elusive.

We are immediately confronted by the question of reception. A review of the extensive discussion of this concept is unnecessary; it is enough to say that by reception I mean an appropriation that effects those changes intended by that which is appropriated. The Leuenberg Agreement would be received when Lutheran and Reformed churches realize and express the unity called for by the document. Reception, as I conceive it, will demand that action be taken by the highest judicatories of the involved churches; but this is not enough. Appropriation must penetrate the life of the church so that congregations as well as judicatories are affected.

At this point it might be helpful to note the kinship in meaning of the notion of reception and the Latin term *auctoritas* as used in pre-Christian Rome. E. D. Watt shows that this term did not originally include *potestas*; it indicated a justifiable exercise of influence rather than a legally constituted use of power (*Authority*, St. Martin's Press, 1982). Can the churches of the Lutheran and Reformed traditions receive the Leuenberg Agreement in this way? Is the document capable of exercising *auctoritas* in our situation and thus producing the results in the United States that have been sought in Europe? My response to these questions will take special note of the three areas of concern identified by the Lutheran Church in America (LCA) convention in 1986: Christology, Eucharist, and predestination. What follows will attempt to deal with the complexity of the task by examining the relevance of the Leuenberg text, the significance of its contexts, the possibility of its employment as pretext, and its relation to a Reformed ecumenical subtext. Let me note two things before moving to these topics. First, I do not speak for the Reformed tradition in America, nor even for my own church. My reflections represent the Reformed perspective in that I am a Reformed theologian who has become something of a veteran warrior in Lutheran–Reformed dialogue.

Second, this is not the first time the relevance of the Leuenberg Agreement for Lutheran–Reformed unity in America has been addressed. Twice in the past the agreement has been part of the Lutheran–Reformed conversation. *An Invitation to Action*, the report of the third dialogue, includes the full text of the document, which it affirms and builds on. Leuenberg also was taken under consideration by the second Lutheran–Reformed consultation (1972-74). Its report indicates that the attempt made to use the agreement as a vehicle for unity failed because of the document's "alleged ambiguities and compromises," its inadequacy for churches in the American culture, and its preoccupation with sixteenth century issues. The report comments: "It is possible that a formal agreement among our churches in America might have been achieved if our group had recommended that Leuenberg be sent to them to be signed." The irony here cannot escape us; the dialogue that has been judged the least productive—some say a failure—formulated the possibility now before us almost fifteen years later. It should also be noted that, for different reasons and under different circumstances, both the second and third series of conversations declined the Leuenberg Agreement as a vehicle for Lutheran–Reformed unity in America. These refusals must be taken into consideration in our appraisal of the agreement. But we need not be bound by them; a fresh look at the Leuenberg Agreement may throw new light on their appropriateness for our situation. After all, that's why we're here.

Now we may return to the question before us and examine the matters of text, context, pretext, and subtext.

TEXTUALITY

In assessing the relevance of the Leuenberg Agreement for America, certain questions arise. What are the inherent merits of the document?

PAUL R. FRIES

Does it have qualities that would suggest its likely reception by both Lutherans and Reformed? An affirmative answer would be merited if four criteria were met: 1) if the agreement took into account traditional church-dividing issues, especially those raised by the LCA convention in 1986 for further investigation, *viz.*, Christology, Eucharist and predestination; 2) if it offered a constructive statement of theology and mission that expressed Lutheran–Reformed unity in a way which both traditions could regard as adequate; 3) if its recommendations were suitable for the American situation; and 4) if its text accomplished all this better than other available documents.

There can be no question that the Leuenberg Agreement attempted to give serious attention to the concerns attendant to the first two criteria. The polemic of the 16th and subsequent centuries was very much on the minds of the document's drafters, and careful attention is given by the drafters to the origins of the divisions that have plagued the churches of the two traditions since that time (LA 5). The Agreement asserts that theological distinctions which once raised walls between Lutheran and Reformed churches should no longer be regarded as church dividing, and certainly not the occasion for the condemnations that sealed the opposition of the traditions (17-27). The condemnations can now be lifted, the document argues, because a fundamental agreement in the gospel is yet visible through the polemical smoke of the period (4). The test of the Augsburg Confession's Article 7 is met. Instances of this are given in its statements on justification by faith, Baptism, and Eucharist (7-16), and in its declaration that the ancient condemnations are no longer in effect (17-27).

All three areas of concern identified by the 1986 convention of the LCA—Christology, Eucharist, and predestination, (subjects of condemnation in the Augsburg Confession, Article 10)—are treated by the Agreement. The statement of common Christological affirmation is brief:

> In the true man Jesus Christ, the eternal Son, and so God himself, has bestowed himself upon lost mankind for its salvation. In the word of promise and in the sacraments, the Holy Spirit, and so God himself, makes the crucified and risen Jesus present to us (21).

70

There is nothing objectionable in the statement from my Reformed perspective. The paragraph stops short of plunging Christology into soteriology, which, in the Reformed view, seems to be a tendency of Lutheran theology. The identification of the action of the Spirit with the presence of Christ wins approbation from the Calvinist camp. But is enough said here? Is the statement not only minimal, but minimalistic? A facile dismissal of deep running issues of history? Here the Leuenberg Agreement suffers from the lack of scholarly support that preceded it and provided its context in Europe, but that is denied to those who would "lift" it from its continental environment. *An Invitation to Action* appears stronger at this point, built as it is on the solid scholarship of *Marburg Revisited* and thus offering a contextualized treatment of the issues (which includes an attempt to contextualize the Leuenberg Agreement).

Christology

The Agreement's second paragraph on Christology invites us to transcend the historically conditioned thought-forms that set Lutheran and Reformed theology in opposition, and to seek ways to preserve the genius of each. The quintessence of Reformed Christology, according to the document, is "to maintain unimpaired the divinity and humanity of Jesus" while that of the Lutheran tradition is "to maintain the unity of Jesus as a person" (22).

Now it is easy to sympathize with the attempt to show the two traditions complementary in regard to their understanding of the incarnation. But I wonder if what is said at this point does not represent a misunderstanding of Reformed Christology. It seems to me that Calvin's teaching that in the Lord's Supper we receive the flesh of Jesus through the work of the Spirit came precisely because of his concern for the unity of the person, despite all the charges of Nestorian tendencies in his thought. The theanthropic person can not be sundered; therefore after the ascension a claim that the flesh of Jesus was everywhere present would violate Calvin's notion of the union of the divine and the human in Christ (*unio hypostatica*). Our salvation depends on being joined to the life, human and divine, of the man Jesus; on receiving him, yes, in the flesh, and also being

PAUL R. FRIES

received by him. In the words of the Heidelberg Catechism, in answer to the question "What does it mean to eat the crucified body of Christ and to drink his poured out blood?":

> Through the Holy Spirit, who lives both in Christ and in us, we are united more and more to Christ's blessed body. And so, although he is in heaven and we are on earth, we are flesh of his flesh, and bone of his bone. And we forever live on and are governed by one Spirit, as members of our body are by one soul (Q. 76).

The Eucharist

Our discussion of Christology has already carried across the threshold of our second concern, the Eucharist. The Lord's Supper is addressed both in section 2 of the Leuenberg Agreement, where our common understanding of the gospel is presented, and in the third part dealing with condemnations. An American Reformed commentator finds little to quibble with in what is said here. The sacramental realism, as I would call it, which identifies Christ as the one imparted through the meal is welcome, as is the early mention of "the word of promise" as the guarantor of his presence (LA 15). The meal as remembrance (*anamnesis*) and eschatological event are also referred to, although these terms are not employed (16). A form of the reception of the elements of communion by those who are unworthy appears: "He thus gives himself unreservedly to all who receive the bread and wine; faith receives the Lord's Supper for salvation, unfaith for judgment" (18).

If Lutherans are surprised that the *manducatio indignorum* can be affirmed by Reformed churches, they are unfamiliar with the teachings of Calvin and the Reformed Confessions. Indeed, the Belgic Confession (1561), approved by Calvin, states:

> In the meantime we err not when we say that what is eaten and drunk by us is the proper and natural body and the proper blood of Christ. . . . This feast is a spiritual table, at which Christ communicates Himself with all His benefits to us, and gives us there to enjoy both Himself and the merits of His suffering and death: nourishing, strengthening and comforting our poor comfortless souls by eating of His flesh, quickening

72

and refreshing them by the drinking of His blood. . . . The ungodly indeed receives the sacrament to his condemnation, but he does not receive the truth of the sacrament, even as Judas and Simon the sorcerer both indeed received the sacrament but not Christ who was signified by it (Art. 35).

The drafters of the Leuenberg Agreement might well conclude on the basis of such evidence that there is concurrence on the meaning of the presence of Jesus in the sacrament, and that the "how question" (*wie-Frage*) ought not be regarded as church dividing.

But here too there is at least one omission that leaves the Reformed theologian less than sanguine about the document's eucharistic theology. For the Calvinist, the "call upon God" (*epiklesis*) is constituitive for the celebration of the Supper, and yet there is no mention of the Holy Spirit in the eucharistic paragraphs. This is no small matter for us; on the one hand it is at the heart of our eucharistic theology, and on the other hand, it is important to our conversation with other bodies, especially the Orthodox. The question of the Holy Spirit in the Eucharist opens to broader issues of pneumatology, for while Calvin has been described as the theologian of the Spirit par excellence, I would characterize his theology not as pneumatological but as fully trinitarian, especially in regard to the works of the Trinity viewed externally to the Trinity (*opera trinitatis ad extra*).

Predestination

This brings us to the last of the trio of special concerns: predestination. The statement made by the Leuenberg Agreement on this craggy doctrine which for many, wrongly so I believe, has become the rock on which Lutheran–Reformed understanding has shipwrecked, is carefully nuanced and would win the approval of most Reformed theologians. While the section is headed "Predestination," it is *election* that is discussed, except in the sentence reading: "The witness of the Scriptures to Christ forbids us to suppose that God has uttered an eternal decree for the final condemnation of specific individuals or of a particular people" (25). One is sorry that the terrible social injustices grounded on the doctrine of predestination were not articulated; the document is in general lacking in its awareness of the connection of theology to issues of social justice. On another matter, this section also would have benefited from a fully trinitarian perspective, especially one placing the work of the Holy Spirit in the foreground, which could have produced a more elegant articulation of the tension between divine initiative and human response.

At this point we may return to the first two criteria for textual reception, viz. that the text of the Leuenberg Agreement would be intrinsically suitable as a vehicle for Lutheran–Reformed unity if it took into account traditional church-dividing issues, especially those raised by the LCA in 1986 for further investigation; and if it offered a constructive statement of theology and mission which expressed Lutheran–Reformed unity in a way which both traditions could regard as adequate. I believe that the agreement offers a solid but overly condensed treatment; and while I see no reason that the Reformed churches in America could not subscribe to most of what is said both in section 2 on the common understanding of the gospel and section 3 regarding doctrinal condemnations of the past, there are important theological issues not satisfactorily represented in the document. These include the *unio hypostatica* in Reformed theology, the *epiklesis*, the role of the Holy Spirit, a trinitarian theological methodology, and a concern for social justice. Some of these issues were dealt with in the background work that preceded the drafting of the document, and some in subsequent discussions, but this material is not before us.

Meanwhile, there are two remaining criteria to be taken into account briefly. Are the recommendations of the Leuenberg Agreement suitable for the American situation? and Does its text accomplish what it does better than other available documents?

The Agreement invites churches to join in making the declaration:

With these statements, church fellowship is declared. The divisions which have barred the way to this fellowship since the 16th century are removed. The participating churches are convinced that they have been put together in the one church of Jesus Christ, and that the Lord liberates them for, and lays upon them the obligation of, common service (34).

Beyond this, implications for church fellowship are drawn. They are certainly worth studying but lack the focus and specificity that would give them promise for our situation in North America. By contrast, *An Invitation to Action*, representing, as it does, the work of American theologians, provides a number of recommendations tailored to the United States.

CONTEXTUALITY

This analysis of the inherent strengths of the Leuenberg Agreement does not settle the question of its applicability to the American situation. Contextual considerations might lead to the conclusion that this document could be received where others, perhaps textually superior, could not. Reception depends on achieving not the best text, but one that is capable of exercising *auctoritas*. Perhaps the best text *is* the one that can achieve reception. Are there contextual factors that might commend the Leuenberg Agreement to us?

A number can be identified. First, one might begin by noting the integrity of the process that produced the document, the scholarly or ecclesial authority of its authors, the situation that elicited it, and its success in, and in some cases beyond, the constituencies for which it was intended. But all this is of the European context. Since both the second and third bilaterals in the United States declined to use the Leuenberg Agreement as an instrument for Lutheran–Reformed unity, it appears that the document's illustrious pedigree was not on those occasions sufficient to warrant its election as the preferred agent of fellowship. Has our situation ripened so that what was apparently not possible in 1974 and 1983 now is?

Second, attention must also be given to the political situation that developed within the uniting Lutheran churches in the years immediately prior to the formation of the Evangelical Lutheran Church in America (ELCA) as this affected the Lutheran response to *An Invitation to Action*, and the current climate in the ELCA. It certainly would not be appropriate for an outsider to attempt to give an account of the complex set of events that occurred before the constituting assembly. I know enough about those difficult days for

Lutherans, however, to realize that *An Invitation to Action* was at the center of a fire storm that caused its recommendations to bear an enormous political freight. It is possible that *An Invitation to Action* and its recommendations will never be free of this burden, that the best course would be to let the report take its place in the archives of lost ecumenical causes and turn to a tested vehicle, such as the Leuenberg Agreement, for Lutheran–Reformed fellowship. Although the Reformed bodies participating in the new conversations have found, or, in the case of the United Church of Christ, are likely to find the recommendations of *An Invitation to Action* perfectly acceptable, the achievement of visible unity might warrant the abandoning of this report in favor of a document that could achieve Lutheran unity for the sake of Lutheran–Reformed unity.

On the other hand, one may discern a trajectory of Lutheran–Reformed conversation in America: beginning with the mandate for the first bilateral in 1961, which produced *Marburg Revisited*; including the second conversation, coming to fruition in the report of the third series; and culminating with two Lutheran and two Reformed bodies entered into fellowship. That such fellowship involving the American Lutheran Church (ALC), American Evangelical Lutheran Church (AELC), Presbyterian Church USA, (PC[USA]) and the Reformed Church in America (RCA) was effected is a blunt fact of history that will not go away. What bearing does this event have on our present discussion? Can it be forgotten, as if nothing occurred? Would the use of an instrument imported from Europe, which calls for less than the action taken by these churches in 1986, compromise commitments made in good faith? If this is a perplexing question for Lutherans, it is no less for Reformed and Presbyterians. After years of courtship, a marriage is finally achieved, only to be annulled—and instead of enjoying the fruits of wedded bliss, we are forced to begin courting the same partner again. Does the Leuenberg Agreement help us with this issue of ecumenical integrity?

Third, special circumstances pertain to relations between the Lutheran church and the United Church of Christ. Because the United Church of Christ differed in several significant ways from the other Reformed bodies participating in the third conversation, separate talks were held between the ALC, LCA, and AELC shortly before the birth of the Evangelical Lutheran Church in America (ELCA). As a result of these and other negotiations on a heads-of-communion basis, agreement was reached that the United Church of Christ would participate in new conversations involving the ELCA, PC[USA], and RCA. Were the Leuenberg Agreement to become an instrument through which the United Church of Christ could stand with the other Reformed churches in the establishment of fellowship with the ELCA, I believe that this might prove to be a contextual factor warranting its employment. However, one would expect it to be made clear how the Leuenberg Agreement could become a bridge between Lutheran and Reformed where *An Invitation to Action* failed.

Fourth, there is concern that Lutheran–Reformed fellowship be set in the broader context of the catholicity of the church. The Leuenberg Agreement would serve us well if it made strong hermeneutic connection with the ecumenical commitments that Reformed and Lutheran churches have made in other venues. Decisions concerning method and substance have been made by the various dialogues, both domestic and international, and a number of recommendations adopted by sponsoring bodies. In addition to bilateral conversations, some of the participating churches are involved in conciliar ecumenism, again both on the national and world levels, as well as in special unity endeavors such as the Consultation on Church Unity (COCU). Certainly no serious ecumenical endeavor can be attempted today apart from a consideration of the Lima document. In my remarks at the first meeting of the Lutheran–Reformed conversation, I appealed for a hermeneutic that would allow us to assess current ecumenical engagement in the light of the reports and decisions made by the churches of our tradition in previous dialogues and in other ecumenical arenas.

Since the churches represented in the current dialogue participate in a variety of ecumenical endeavors, and since these endeavors draw us into conversation with bodies of vastly divergent ecclesiologies, the vehicle effecting Lutheran–Reformed unity should also hold open the door to fellowship with other churches. Would the reception of the Leuenberg Agreement inhibit or facilitate conversation with the churches embracing the historical episcopacy? With the "free churches"? The Church catholic is a contextual factor of the first magnitude that must not fall from the sight of those engaged in bilateral dialogue.

A PRETEXT?

One's ability to make a final determination on the suitability of the Leuenberg Agreement for reception in our churches is clouded by the evidence that there are strong voices in the ELCA who oppose Lutheran–Reformed pulpit and table fellowship, that for them such fellowship would confuse and even hinder what they regard as a growing relationship with the Roman Catholic Church; and that these voices successfully blocked the adoption of the recommendations based on *An Invitation to Action* at the LCA convention in 1986. Reformed participants in the new round of conversation, who not only have followed the fire storms concerning *An Invitation to Action* in the press but also have been told bitter tales by sympathetic Lutherans, can only wonder why the Leuenberg Agreement is now before us. Unhappily, a hermeneutic of suspicion now colors our perceptions. Is the current consideration of the Leuenberg Agreement a delaying action? Would offering it to the Lutheran and Reformed churches as an instrument for fellowship be a sop thrown to those from the ALC and AELC who were disturbed by the LCA response to *An Invitation to Action*? The Leuenberg Agreement is regarded by some as a paper tiger that has accomplished very little in Europe. If the Leuenberg Agreement is more than a pretext, this must be textually and/or contextually demonstrated by its advocates. Only in this way will the Reformed hermeneutic of suspicion be overcome.

THE REFORMED ECUMENICAL SUBTEXT

To raise the question of pretext is not to suggest that it is inappropriate for the churches of a given tradition to bring to bilateral or counciliar conversation an ecumenical agenda based on their theology and ecclesiology. Every ecumenical text offered to the churches for reception reflects the subtexts brought to the formative discussions by the participants. A pretext is ecumenical bad faith; a subtext is the equipment of the ecumenical saint.

Here I would fault my own tradition. I think we have been remarkably guileless in ecumenical conversation, but not because of virtue; true, we have rarely used pretexts, but perhaps this is because we have carried with us undernourished subtexts. In the 1950s, at the Princeton assembly of the World Alliance of Reformed Churches, an ecumenical stance was adopted which, I believe, continues to inform and weaken our subtext. Our position was, briefly stated, that Reformed unity was subordinate to and in the service of the quest for a more comprehensive fellowship among the churches. The extremely low profile of World Alliance of Reformed Churches in the world Church in comparison with, say, the Lutheran World Federation is evidence of this policy at work. We have thus become a protean figure in ecumenical dialogue; when in conversation with Baptists we tend to sound like Baptists, with Methodists like Methodists, with the Anglicans, like Anglicans (albeit low church Anglicans!). We react to the ecumenical issues voiced by those churches who define the ecumenical agenda; the Orthodox, the Lutheran, and to some degree the Roman Catholic. I believe this posture, as gracious as it may appear, is misguided. It deprives us of our own sense of self, and other churches of our contributions. My appeal is for a sharper Reformed profile and, perhaps, a bit more Calvinistic pugnacity in the ecumenical arena.

In this spirit let me conclude by saying that the relevance of the Leuenberg Agreement for America, as viewed from a Reformed perspective, is conditional. There are certain doctrinal questions such as trinity, Spirit, *epiklesis*, the *unio hypostatica*, and social justice that are not adequately treated in the document. There are also the contextual issues of the document's catholicity, the fellowship established between Lutheran and Reformed bodies in 1986, and the suitability of the agreement to respond to the ELCA–UCC question. There is the suspicion that the document is being used as a pretext. If these concerns are successfully dealt with, its promise for reception will be greatly enhanced. Leuenberg may become the light in which the key to unity is found, but not without a continuing and thorough search.

6

The Leuenberg Agreement in the North American Context

I wish to speak on behalf of the Leuenberg Agreement as a means toward church fellowship between Lutherans and Reformed. In this regard, I believe that the topic assigned to me for this conference— Leuenberg in the North American context—is ill-conceived. The question of the North American context is not finally a proper or a helpful one to raise in reflecting on Leuenberg today. My reason for this assertion is theological.

PROPER AND IMPROPER CRITERIA FOR CHURCH FELLOWSHIP

Theologically, as Marc Lienhard has pointed out, Leuenberg approaches the question of church fellowship between Lutherans and Reformed in a time-honored way: by focusing on gospel and sacraments which are the marks of the church and the sufficient basis for "the true unity of the Christian church" (Augsburg Confession, article 7). From Marburg (1529), where Luther and Zwingli separated over the Lord's Supper; to Wittenberg (1536), where Luther extended the hand of fellowship to Martin Bucer and the Upper Germans even though the Lutheran doctrine of the Lord's Supper was not accepted as a whole; to Arnoldshain (1957), where distinguished theologians proposed church fellowship on the basis of the investigation of the marks of the church in light of current scholarship on the New Testament: in all of these instances, the marks of the church have been the proper focus in ecumenical discussions between Lutherans and Reformed. "The Reformation churches," asserts Lienhard, "would have had to yield their self-understanding . . . if they sought to create fellowship simply by organizational means or to leave it in a fog of friendly disposition"[1]—or, one might add these days, to leave it in a fog of unfriendly disposition. Lutherans and Reformed have not done so. They have focused the question of fellowship on fundamental theological criteria, gospel and sacraments, derived from their fundamental theological identity and not from the question of context. This is the way it should be done and this is the approach that Leuenberg takes.

Lienhard, in fact, goes on to raise a specific warning against accepting other criteria for church fellowship: namely, "a specific historical situation, a political event, or a certain kind of organization."[2] If these other criteria are operating when Leuenberg is assessed, then the theological criteria of gospel and sacraments—the *satis est*, "it is enough" of the Reformation and Augsburg (article 7)—are compromised and subordinated. Since these improper contextual criteria of specific historical situation, politics, and organization are cited by those who oppose fellowship among Lutherans and Reformed—fellowship based, in part, on the achievement of Leuenberg—I question the implications of the topic that I have been assigned. A debate over what Leuenberg says about gospel and sacraments may too easily get lost in secondary matters, even if they are matters of burning interest to those who raise them.

Relevance

Let me be more specific. I have heard the argument, plain and simple, that Leuenberg is not relevant to the North American context at the present time. This is the first extraneous criterion of "specific historical situation." The commonly cited source for this argument is the second round of discussions of the Lutheran–Reformed dialogue. Now round two does present this argument but in words that are intentionally vague. It speaks of "some" objecting to "alleged ambiguities and compromises"[3] in Leuenberg; of "others" concerned about our "pluralistic society"; and of "still others" worried about the contrast between settling sixteenth century disputes on the Lord's Supper and the urgent task of confessing Christ in relation to contemporary issues facing America. These are all different issues, fired at the reader like buckshot. The actual number and identity of the participants who had these problems are not clear. What we do know is that Leuenberg was new at the time of the discussion. It did not have the stature it has since acquired. We know also that the debate among the Lutherans, caused by the raging conflict in the Missouri Synod, was a crucial, perhaps even preeminent factor in the second round.

By the third round, circumstances were quite different. Although a full participant, the Missouri Synod now was less an active player than an observer, submitting a minority report. And Leuenberg, by this time, had been widely accepted. In the third round, Leuenberg, along with *Marburg Revisited*, was "reaffirmed"[4]—a significant word. No longer were concerns expressed about the North American context. Indeed, what was reaffirmed was the long-standing tendency of the Lutheran–Reformed dialogue to take seriously the Reformation heritage and the international scene. Just as it had been proper in the first round of discussions to revisit Marburg— that is, to be concerned about the sixteenth-century disputes and speak to them—so in the third round Leuenberg was considered relevant. This was the true conclusion of the Lutheran–Reformed dialogue in line with its basic tendency from 1963. The vague charges of round two were the unfortunate exceptions to the dialogue, not the rule.

And, indeed—speaking now more generally—why should the North American context be a question, especially in the years since the end of the third round of the Lutheran–Reformed dialogue? We should see how our fellow Lutheran churches in other parts of the world have acted and we should learn from them. The Leuenberg

Agreement was adopted by the United Evangelical Lutheran Church in Argentina in 1986, following the lead of other churches in South America. Leuenberg had also had an impact on the relationship between the Batak Lutheran churches and the Reformed churches established by the Dutch mission to Indonesia. It is affecting the process of wider church union in Indonesia. These churches have not raised the issue of the third-world context. On the contrary, Leuenberg has become a truly international agreement involving over half the Lutherans in the world in pulpit and altar fellowship with Reformed and Presbyterian churches. Such international agreements based on Reformation principles—and there are precious few such principles—truly serve the global unity of Christians. To raise the question of the North American context courts the danger of parochial self-centeredness and sectarianism.

This question of context seems odder when one considers our close ties to Europe, where the agreement was conceived. Europeans took part in this conference. Leaders of our churches are trained in Europe. In his very first month as bishop, Herbert Chilstrom, accompanied by his ecumenical advisor, went to Europe. Last December, when William Rusch announced the trip on a visit to the faculty at Luther Northwestern Seminary in St. Paul, he called it a great ecumenical sign.

We Lutherans base the faith and practice of our own church on the Augsburg Confession. Our seminary students pore over it year after year. It was conceived in Europe. We teach our children Luther's *Small Catechism*, written in Europe. The point is obvious: What makes a document significant is its ability to transcend its origins. Leuenberg has demonstrated that ability. It has that rare historic power to gather Christians in ecumenical relationship.

Political Issues

I have also heard *political* arguments against church fellowship between Lutherans and Reformed. It is said, for example, that church fellowship in North America should be determined by the question of whether Lutherans should identify even more than they have with what is commonly called "mainline, liberal Protestantism" in this secular, pluralistic society. This question is usually linked to another: whether our ecumenical orientation should be toward Protestant churches or toward the Anglican–Catholic tradition. For many of those Lutherans who are contemptuous of various forms of Protestantism, the Anglican–Catholic tradition—and I define this broadly—has become a nostalgic ideal almost beyond criticism; its catchwords are the characteristics of catholic Christianity.

Now I do not believe for a moment that the Anglican-Catholic tradition has escaped the forces of secularism anymore than have Protestant denominations. The entire church faces the same challenges posed by modernity. Serious questions are raised by the eagerness with which American churches have adopted partisan political stands since the 1960s. And mainline, liberal denominations nowadays are open to close, critical scrutiny.

Perhaps the fact that we Lutherans (I do not speak for the Reformed) are a denomination in statistical decline reflects the judgment of many that the world is too much with us. Carl Braaten has recently complained that whereas the charge against Lutheranism in the past involved the twin accusations of "pietism and quietism," the problems now are "secularism and activism."[5] These are serious charges. Braaten and other critics such as Richard John Neuhaus and Paul Hinlicky are on to something very important. Their criticisms need to be thoroughly discussed as the ELCA seeks to develop a theological identity.

The point of my comments on the issue of secularization is this: political calculation about a denomination's role among other denominations, the personal political prejudices of individuals, and the special political interests of organized groups within the Lutheran church should not be the basis for determining efforts toward church fellowship. They go beyond (or shall I say beneath) the *satis est*, the "it is enough" of Reformation teaching. And besides, what does it indicate about the ecumenical enterprise if politics is allowed so much influence in our deliberations and strategy? I agree with Wilfred M. McClay, a historian at Tulane University and a keen observer of the current trend toward politicization in the broad ecumenical scene, who makes this warning:

This ecumenism is increasingly built around specific positions on political and social issues, in which leftist Protestants, Catholics, and Jews gravitate together in order to align themselves against conservative Protestants, Catholics, and Jews. In other words, it is an ecumenism based upon the rise of unbelief, the attenuation of tradition, and the primacy of politics—an ecumenism which follows the concerns of the public square rather than informing them.[6]

This is a very serious matter for ecumenical theology. The question of politics in ecumenism must be attended to carefully. I believe we must guard against it.

Naturally, I wish that everyone thought the way I do. But I know that they do not. And I know that there is much that must be given up for the sake of the unity of the church. This is one reason why I have recently come to appreciate the LCA's 1982 statement, *Ecumenism: A Lutheran Commitment*. It affirms that ecumenism "does not see progress in one area as competitive with advancement in another. Each individual gain with other Christians should be welcomed by all who are ecumenically committed" (Guideline 5). To have ecumenical relations with other churches is not to count the number of Republicans or Democrats, objectivists or subjectivists, sincere or insincere, moral or immoral, orthodox or unorthodox, right or wrong in those churches. What we are dealing with here is a matter of the public confession of the church. Lutherans above all should be alert to this. We are not now and never have been Donatists who make the church dependent on the personal qualities of its membership or ministry.

Church Government

Finally, there is the third improper criterion of "a certain kind of organization." I have heard this argument too. I have heard that church unity should be measured by the presence of an episcopal system of government in a three-fold structure of ministry. These are seen by some as a "sign," though not a guarantee, of the unity of the church. I refer, of course, to *Baptism, Eucharist and Ministry*, the document that has been so significant in the North American context for some, influential Lutherans—Lutherans who, by the way, never seem to raise the contextual question in relation to the non-American aspects of its compositional history. There is at least one special interest group in the ELCA, with heavy representation in Pennsylvania, that has called for the immediate adoption of *BEM*. But is church organization a criterion of the Reformation? And must church fellowship be measured by this standard? Among us Lutherans, the answer to both questions has been and must continue to be emphatically *no*.

And I must say that I am disturbed by any trend in ecumenism that seeks to move from the marks of the church (*notae Ecclesiae*), to the marks of Christendom (*notae Christianorum*). Among us, the marks of gospel and sacraments take precedence over even the notes of unity, holiness, catholicity, and apostolicity—particularly when these latter are asserted to be institutionally incarnate. Further, history from Ignatius of Antioch teaches that such a trend signals most often an unwarranted, triumphalist extension of the incarnational principle into church organization, that is, into ecclesiology and ministry. The claim that we are only talking about signs and not guarantees does not make me secure, especially when the issue of the visible unity of the church is so often tied in contemporary ecumenical theology to the highly debatable political judgment that the church's survival in a modern, pluralistic age depends on church unity.[7]

I remain haunted by what Luther said so long ago about what signs to look for when one seeks the church:

> The church is a high, deep, hidden thing which one may neither perceive nor see, but must grasp only by faith, through baptism, sacrament, and word. Human doctrine, ceremonies, tonsures, long robes, miters and all the pomp . . . only lead far away from it . . . still less are they signs of the church. Naked children, men, women, farmers, citizens who possess no tonsures, miters, or priestly vestments also belong to the church.[8]

Luther's is a radical, inclusive vision of the signs of the church. It may offend some because it has today the same ability to startle and make one think about fundamentals that it had in the sixteenth century. Its ecumenical potential, however, is enormous. It is a vision that we dare not give up. The hiddenness of the church, of which it speaks, is grounded in the hiddenness of the gospel in the world—known only through the crucified Christ. We should seek the signs of hiddenness that join all human creatures. Impressive edifices, tempting though they be for our minds and passions (especially the minds and passions of the ordained clergy), do not lead us to God. Human limitedness, human finitude, the inevitable tragedies of life lead us to God. We learn what the church is when we preach Christ crucified (1 Cor. 1:23). As Eberhard Jüngel has recently observed, reflecting on Luther's *Bondage of the Will*:

> The human *intellectus* judges according to the visible appearance . . .
> "is a respecter of persons" . . . Conversely, what marks God's better
> sight is that it is directed toward the nothing (become articulable as such
> only in the shape of the crucifixion of Jesus Christ). Accordingly, within
> what is created, God's sight observes what is defined more by nothing
> than by being, more by absence than the total possession of possibilities
> . . . There in God's eyes . . . the sinner, totally unworthy of love,
> crooked and ugly, becomes upright in a new righteousness and con-
> formable to God.[9]

Whenever the church has proclaimed its structural visibility as a redeemed community and defined its ministry as the prerogative of an elite class, it has usually sinned both by thinking that it is somehow morally superior to the rest of the world and by treating its theology as a guaranteed ideology. The true church is hidden in the world because it is made up of the people of the world—sinners all, "totally unworthy of love," yet loved, embraced in the gospel.

There was a Lutheran in Pennsylvania, long ago, who knew this lesson well; he especially knew its application to the minds and passions of the ordained clergy. His name was Henry Melchoir Muhlenberg. Writing in 1779 to his Episcopalian contemporaries in his official capacity as Senior Minister of the United Lutheran clergy in North America, he had this to say about theologies of church structure and their relation to the task of ministry: "Experience shows that neither Episcopal, nor Ministerial or Presbyterial Ordination doth infuse any natural or supernatural Gifts or Qualities, otherwise we should not find so many counterfeited ministers, refined Hypocrites, and grievous Wolves in the Christian Church on Earth, instead of true and faithful Shepherds." [10] Now there is an observation for those in the Reformation tradition and the American religious tradition (and also for those among us who continue to love the spirit of the eighteenth century) that certainly goes *ad fontes*, "to the sources."

This is why I am concerned: If these improper criteria become the measure of church fellowship, then the actual claims of Leuenberg can be misread or the agreement may be turned into a controversial symbol or flash-point for other things.

THE LEUENBERG AGREEMENT

I would now like to turn more properly to the matter of Leuenberg itself: first to make some brief observations about the nature of ecumenical agreements and Lutheran–Reformed relations; and then to discuss at length the content of the Leuenberg Agreement.

The Nature of Agreements

First, ecumenical agreements. Leuenberg is an ecumenical agreement. Ecumenical agreements are things that are finally, simply *there*. They are official documents, completed, usually sparse in expression. Rarely do they try to reinvent the wheel: that is, to say something brand new. Usually they do not contain traditional words and phrases dear to a specific group. They are more neutral in expression. We need to remember these simple facts about ecumenical agreements.

Second, let us also remember some basic facts about modern Lutheran–Reformed relations. These have been characterized both by the process of official, long-standing dialogue and by the efficient achievement of agreements. The dialogues have usually had a set amount of time and a limited budget. Their shared heritage, schooling, and theological literature have allowed Lutheran and Reformed

89

partners to focus quickly. And so we have had specific documents to work with from these meetings. We have had ecumenical agreements. And with agreements comes controversy. This is natural. But it can leave the false impression that the ecumenical relationship entered and under scrutiny is not as solid as would be one based on dialogue with those churches on the ecumenical scene that have the ability to draw the most widespread media attention.

This impression is false. Just the opposite is the case. As George Lindbeck, prominent Lutheran theologian and one of the guiding figures on the Lutheran–Roman Catholic dialogue, stated in lectures delivered at Union Seminary in Virginia in 1985:

> As I suppose we are all aware, the Reformed–Lutheran discussions have attracted less attention both inside and outside the churches than have the dialogues with Rome or even the Lutheran conversations with the Anglicans. Perhaps this was partly because their conclusions were expected. After all, most people already believed that the historic Reformed–Lutheran disagreements no longer warrant division.

Lindbeck is right. He also observes that "the theological and liturgical dimensions" of the eucharistic controversies between Lutherans and Reformed "are no longer in themselves divisive . . ." Lindbeck calls Luther and Calvin "high sacramental realists" in the present three-way conversation of Lutheran, Reformed, and Roman Catholic, and when he states bluntly that, "if Augustine did not contradict transubstantiation, neither does John Calvin," he witnesses to the enormous range of convergence in the ecumenical enterprise today.[11] In short, the ecumenical relations of Lutherans and Reformed are healthy and dynamic and are very much part of the current ecumenical scene.

Now let us look at the content of Leuenberg itself. I wish to propose the following thesis: The Leuenberg Agreement is relevant to the North American context, as it is relevant in the international context, because its claims for church fellowship, grounded in gospel and sacraments, are theologically valid according to the enduring Lutheran standard of ecumenical outreach.

Please notice, if you will, that last phrase: according to the enduring Lutheran standard of ecumenical outreach. I take as that standard neither my private opinion nor the requirements of Lutheran bodies that would not be accepted by this gathering: say, for example, the standards of the Missouri Synod or the Wisconsin Synod. I refer to the standard for ecumenical relations expressed in our confessions and in contemporary representative documents such as that of the Working Group of the Lutheran World Federation on "the Interrelations between [sic] the Various Bilateral Dialogues," chaired by Robert Marshall and published in 1977. Bilateral dialogues, according to that report, are "not intended to produce a comprehensive treatment of all subjects but progress towards practical, bilateral clarification in each case." [12]

This standard is a modest one. It does not require each dialogue to reconceive Christology or the Hellenization thesis; to define the metaphysical nature of a body's presence or (God forbid) predestination; or to resolve some other grand issue. The agreements of dialogues do not make those type of claims. On the contrary, in an ecumenical agreement from a dialogue, one is likely to read disclaimers of any attempt at grand, all-compassing systematic assertions. For example, consider this sensible disclaimer regarding the Lord's Supper—that most thorny of issues:

> Our conversations have persuaded us of both the legitimacy and the limits of theological efforts to explore the mystery of Christ's presence in the sacrament. We are also persuaded that no single vocabulary or conceptual framework can be adequate, exclusive or final in this theological enterprise. [13]

This statement, taken from the third Lutheran–Roman Catholic dialogue, is a typical, economical statement of ecumenical agreement. This, incidentally, is the most inclusive statement of the American Lutheran–Roman Catholic dialogues concerning the Lord's Supper. It is as far as the dialogue goes. What weightier standard, one might ask, is required by Lutherans of the Lutheran–Reformed fellowship?

Now with this modest standard of measurement in mind, hear what the Leuenberg Agreement says about the Lord's Supper:

> In the Lord's Supper the risen Jesus Christ imparts himself in his body and blood, given up for all, through his word of promise with bread and

wine. He thus gives himself unreservedly to all who receive the bread and wine; faith receives the Lord's Supper for salvation, unfaith for judgment (18).

Further:

> In the true man Jesus Christ, the eternal Son, and so God himself, has bestowed himself upon lost mankind for its salvation. In the word of the promise and in the sacraments, the Holy Spirit, and so God himself, makes the crucified and risen Jesus present to us. (21)

I submit that the essentials are here. It is a statement of ecumenical agreement. It has received a most positive evaluation from the LWF Working Group on bilateral dialogues:

> [The Leuenberg Agreement] insists firmly on the christological prerequisite of Christ's self-emptying by means of the incarnation and draws the necessary conclusions from this for the doctrine of the Lord's Supper (*finitum capax infiniti* [The finite is capable of the infinite]).[14]

The Committee goes on to say that the Lutheran view of the bodily presence is given strong emphasis so that there is sufficient recognition of the oral eating (*manducatio oralis*) and the eating by the unworthy (*manducatio indignorum*) to ensure that Christ's presence is acknowledged in the external sacramental act. Thus communion with Christ and the eating and drinking are one event.

Now there are some individuals who still have questions. One American Lutheran writer, who is otherwise very sympathetic to Leuenberg, has made this demand recently in the *Lutheran Forum*: "We need detailed discussions with the Lutheran churches in Germany about the doctrinal and practical results of fifteen years of Leuenberg [*sic*] before we simply take its adequacy for granted."[15] This writer wants to avoid or somehow to counter "the internalization and subjectivization of religion" that he perceives around him. He seems to believe that a doctrine of the sacrament is going to accomplish this. Another writer, in the same issue of *Lutheran Forum*, has said that when it comes to the question of fellowship with the

Reformed, Lutherans need to protect their "principle of sacramentality." This principle, in his view, signals "the divorce between Lutherans and protestantism" because for protestantism, the Lutheran stance is "an idolatrous identification of the divine and the human."[16] On the basis of this "objective" principle of sacramentality, he then goes on to make this proposal concerning Lutheran–Reformed fellowship in the form of rhetorical questions:

> What gift do we give the Reformed denominations unless we help them to re-confessionalize and become the church again? What would be the meaning of 'altar and pulpit' fellowship with denominations whose pulpits remain undisciplined, where the sacraments remain marginal?[17]

We Lutherans, you see, know what the church truly is. We alone have the truth. All should listen to us.

For all the world, I could swear that I heard the strains of the "Missouri Waltz" in these types of claims. It seems that the old American Lutheran preoccupation with extra-confessional doctrinal agreements and purity in practice is raising its ugly head yet again. This courts the danger of a doctrinal precisionism that the nineteenth and early twentieth century history of American Lutheranism should have taught us to leave behind. Precisely how high do some want to build the fearful wall of purity in doctrine and practice? And why does the wall seem to be built for some, but not for others? I would rather commend to you the faithful and generous appraisal of the LWF Working Group.

Standing behind Leuenberg on this matter is Arnoldshain. That is where the real breakthrough comes. Signing Arnoldshain were among others: Bizer, Bornkamm, Brunner, Gollwitzer, Iwand, Jeremias, Kaesemann, v. Loewenich, Michel, Niesel, Schlink, Schweitzer, Vogel, Weber, Wolf. In that list are the mentors of many American Lutheran faculty. And even conservative Lutherans in Europe, such as Karl-Hermann Kandler, writing as recently as 1982, have had to admit that what Arnoldshain said about the Lord's Supper represents the *opinio communis* of New Testament scholarship.[18] Any comparison of Arnoldshain and Leuenberg shows their close similarity.

Particularly important in this regard is the Fifth Thesis of Arnoldshain:

> Therefore, what happens in the Lord's Supper is not adequately described, . . .
> (d) when it is taught that there are two parallel but separate processes which take place, one an eating on the part of the body and the other an eating on the part of the soul:
> (e) when it is taught that the eating on the part of the body as such saves one, or that participation in the body and blood of Christ is a purely mental or spiritual matter.[19]

Once again: Communion with Christ and eating and drinking are asserted to be one event.

On the gospel Leuenberg states:

> Whoever puts his trust in the gospel is justified in God's sight for the sake of Jesus Christ, and set free from the accusation of the law. In daily repentance and renewal, he lives within the fellowship in praise of God and in service to others, in the assurance that God will bring his kingdom in all its fullness. In this way, God creates new life, and plants in the midst of the world the seed of a new humanity. (10)

"Whoever puts his trust in the gospel"—Robert W. Bertram in an essay for the Lutheran–Roman Catholic dialogue on justification makes it clear that Lutherans have not demanded a certain conceptuality, but that salvation be proclaimed *sola fide*.[20] This is the standard for ecumenical agreements recognized as valid by Lutherans. It is fulfilled in Leuenberg. What more is needed?

Satis est; it is enough. What more is needed? How much will be enough for the Lutheran critics of Leuenberg? (Are we really, for example, to take up the issue of predestination in our new "theological conversations" with the Reformed?) Let us not replace the Galesburg Rule[21] of the nineteenth century with a Chicago Rule here at the end of the twentieth century—the most ecumenical century the church has ever known. Let us not become the sectarians we once were. We have enough to repent of already.

Indeed, if you remember anything from the historical heritage of American Lutheranism, remember Henry Melchoir Muhlenberg, the patriarch of the eastern Lutheran traditions that became embodied in the former LCA. At the creation of the first *ministerium* of Lutheran clergy at a meeting held in Pennsylvania in 1748—a meeting that one Lutheran historian has called, "the most important event in the history of the Lutheran Church in America"[22]—Muhlenberg invited Reformed leaders to be present at the deliberations, to take part in worship, and to participate in the first service of ordination.[23] Now that is the proud tradition we can take possession of again.

In conclusion: To ask the question of the Leuenberg Agreement in the North American context is ill-conceived. The proper measure of the agreement, like that of any ecumenical agreement, is gospel and sacraments. I challenge anyone to show on the basis of scripture and confession that Leuenberg errs. I challenge anyone to show that the sufficient basis for the true unity of the church, broad and generous yet sharply defined, has not been carefully respected in this document. And if you believe that you have such a basis for criticism, then explain it in detail and apply it consistently to all the ecumenical agreements into which we American Lutherans have entered in recent years.

Notes

1. Marc Lienhard, "Church Fellowship through the Leuenberg Agreement," *Lutheran World* 21 (1974): 333.
2. *Ibid.*
3. James E. Andrews and Joseph A. Burgess, ed. *An Invitation to Action* (Philadelphia: Fortress, 1984), 56.
4. *Ibid.,* p. 16.
5. Carl Braaten, "We Have a Bishop," *Dialog* 26 (1987); 162.
6. Wilfred M. McClay, "Christian Unity," *Commentary* 86 (July 1988): 72. This is a review essay of Richard John Neuhaus, *The Catholic Moment: The Paradox of the Church in the Postmodern World* (New York: Harper & Row, 1987).
7. Consider this alarmist judgment: "This unity [of the church] is a matter of life or death for Christendom at a time when faith in God and His Christ are most seriously threatened by a worldwide militant atheism, and by a relativistic skepticism even in those countries where atheism is not yet a state religion." Heinrich Fries and Karl Rahner, *Unity of the Churches: An Actual Possibility*, trans. Ruth and Eric Gritsch (Philadelphia and New York: Fortress and Paulist, 1983), 1. An effective rejoinder to this claim is provided by the late Harold Ditmanson: "I think it is very doubtful whether the existence of separated churches has anything to do with modern unbelief. Disaffected persons with whom I

have spoken refer to the loss of the sense of the sacred, but never to the dividedness of the churches. A dozen books within easy reach of my desk analyze the phenomenon of unbelief or the 'post-Christian era' (John Courtney Murray, *The Problem of God*; Hans Urs von Balthasar, *The God Question and Modern Man*; Arend T. Van Leeuwen, *Christianity in World History*; David L. Edwards, *Religion and Change*; Leslie Neubigin, *Honest Religion for Secular Man*; Allan D. Galloway, *Faith in a Changing Culture*; Langdon Gilkey, *Naming the Whirlwind* and *Reaping the Whirlwind*, etc.). Every scholar deals at length with secularization, technology, and the breakdown of traditional categories of thought and patterns of conduct. But not one ever refers to separated denominations" ("A Response to the Fries-Rahner Proposal for Church Unity," *Lutheran Quarterly,* I [1987]: 385).

8. LW, 41, 211.

9. Eberhard Jüngel, *The Freedom of a Christian: Luther's Significance for Contemporary Theology*, tr. Roy A. Harrisville (Minneapolis: Augsburg, 1988), p. 37.

10. *The Journals of Henry Melchoir Muhlenberg*, ed. Theodore G. Tappert and John W. Doberstein, 3 vols. (Philadelphia: Muhlenberg Press, 1942-1958): 3: 256.

11. These lectures were published as "The Reformation Heritage and Christian Unity," *Lutheran Quarterly,* 2 (Winter 1988), 477-502.

12. *Ecumenical Relations of the Lutheran World Federation*: Report of the Working Group on the Interrelations between the Various Bilateral Dialogues (Geneva: LWF, 1977), #91. (Hereafter cited as *Ecumenical Relations.*)

13. Paul C. Empie and T. Austin Murphy, eds. *Lutherans and Catholics in Dialogue I-III* (Minneapolis: Augsburg, n.d.), III: 196-197.

14. *Ecumenical Relations* #87.

15. David A. Yeago, "On Declining the Invitation: Lutheran–Reformed Dialogue III and the Doctrine of the Eucharist," *Lutheran Forum* 22 (1988): 28.

16. Paul R. Hinlicky, "The Crisis in American Lutheranism Today," *Lutheran Forum* 22 (1988): 10.

17. *Ibid.,* 11.

18. Karl-Hermann Kandler, *Christi Leib und Blut. Studien zur gegenwaertigen lutherischen Abendmahlslehre* [Arbeiten zur Geschichte und Theologie des Luthertums], N.F. Bd. 2 (Hanover: Lutherisches Verlagshaus, 1982): 116-117. Cited in Joseph Burgess, "The Lutheran–Reformed Dialogue in the United States," *Currents in Theology and Mission* 14 (1987): 122.

19. Eugene Skibbe, *Protestant Agreement on the Lord's Supper* (Minneapolis: Augsburg, 1968), 92.

20. George Anderson, T. Austin Murphy, and Joseph A. Burgess, eds. *Justification by Faith* (Minneapolis: Augsburg 1985), 172-84.

21. The Galesburg Rule was drafted by Charles P. Krauth of the General Council in 1872. It stated that Lutheran pulpits are for Lutheran ministers only and that Lutheran altars are for Lutheran communicants only. See *The Lutherans in North America*, ed. E. Clifford Nelson (Philadelphia: Fortress Press, 1975), 311-3.

22. August L. Graebner, *Geschichte der Lutherischen Kirche in Amerika* (St. Louis: Concordia, 1982), 313.

23. See *Documentary History of the Evangelical Lutheran Ministerium of Pennsylvania and Adjacent States*; Proceedings of the Annual Conventions from 1748 to 1821 (Philadelphia: Board of Publication of the General Council of the Evangelical Lutheran Church, 1898), 3-23. I am grateful to Professor Todd Nichol of Luther Northwestern Theological Seminary for this reference.

7

The Leuenberg Agreement in the North American Context

My assignment—though Professor Sundberg disapproves it—is to consider the appropriateness of the Leuenberg Agreement as an instrument of Lutheran–Reformed fellowship on the American scene. The question of Lutheran–Reformed fellowship as *such* is of course a different question—and, if I may say so, some of Sundberg's difficulty may stem from a failure to distinguish these two questions. Moreover, since I have the brief for the negative on the first question, and since I have been teaching in Pennsylvania, I must ask you not to attribute any position to me on the second. Indeed, I am a living Lutheran–Reformed fellowship, having once served simultaneously as a Lutheran pastor and as an ordained elder of a Reformed denomination.

WHAT LEUENBERG IS AND IS NOT

Responsible discussion of our question demands, of course, a clear grasp of what precisely the Agreement is—a stipulation which, while it may seem obvious, is not always observed in American discussion.

Regularly we proceed as if the Agreement were the final report of a standard ecumenical dialogue, in which the questions historically dividing two confessions had been taken up and resolved, and which could then provide the theological basis for ecclesial actions establishing fellowship between those confessions. But Leuenberg is no such thing; it is rather itself an actual contract of fellowship. As André Birmelé has written: "The enterprise is not to formulate an ensemble of theses explicating theological consensus to the previously controverted points, but actually to establish and realize communion between the two traditions."[1] Indeed, Leuenberg is so far from being the report of an interconfessional dialogue of the usual format, that on most matters that might be supposed to be in need of discussion between Lutherans and Reformed generally, the Agreement has nothing whatever to say.

It is unfortunate, therefore, that *An Invitation to Action* decisively refers to Leuenberg as the place where consensus is supposed to have been achieved on questions that might divide Reformed and Lutherans generally.[2] It simply will not do to proceed as if Leuenberg were the successful dialogue on the basis of which ecclesial action might proceed. Rather, if American Lutherans think that the Leuenberg Agreement provides a satisfactory instrument of Lutheran–Reformed reconciliation, there is only one course of action appropriate to this instrument: Lutheran bodies must just sign it. That is, we must do what *An Invitation to Action* does *not* propose. Thereby we will enter "pulpit and altar fellowship" with a substantial number of Reformed bodies around the world. But we will not be in new fellowship with anyone in America. And then we will have to wait to see if any Reformed bodies in America at some point also adhere to Leuenberg.

So to the material question: Can the Leuenberg Agreement provide a satisfactory instrument of Lutheran–Reformed pulpit and altar fellowship in the United States? Whether in itself or as the working subtext of *An Invitation to Action*? And it is the Agreement itself which is in question; the Lutheran–Reformed dialogues which have been instituted within the Leuenberg fellowship are interesting contributions to the body of ecumenical results, but it is the Agreement that is special and may be a specific instrument of American Lutheran–Reformed fellowship. The decisive characteristic of Leuenberg is what it does not take up at all. There is no ecclesiology whatsoever. The ministry is not discussed. Nor is even the specifically *reforming* doctrine of "justification" itself noted: the relevant paragraph of Leuenberg reproduces Augustana 4; Apology 4 is ignored.

How are we to explain Leuenberg's omission of all this? Part of the explanation is, of course, the dialogues that preceded Leuenberg. But again the scope of these is strikingly limited at the same time that their depth in a few matters is impressive.

TWO SOURCES OF AGREEMENT AT LEUENBERG

Leuenberg itself provides the answer, in its third and fourth paragraphs: it is shared *history* that has brought the signatories together, and has taught them, in advance of doctrinal discussion, that their differences are not divisive as they once were thought to be. And as we read the trail of documents and commentary, it becomes clear what strands of history thus made the old differences appear in a new light.

There were two. There was first the German *Kirchenkampf* (church conflict). And there was second, to quote Marc Lienhard, "ecumenical confrontation" with a partner that both German Lutheranism and German Reformed Christianity have experienced as more different from each than is either from the other: the Roman Catholic Church.[3] At this fundamental level it is thus most doubtful that Leuenberg can be an appropriate instrument of Lutheran–Reformed fellowship in the United States, since what enabled the Agreement was not newly worked out agreement, but two trails of historical experience, neither of which is ours.

First, the *Kirchenkampf* confronted German-speaking Reformed and Lutheran Christianity with one another's virtues and sins, and with shared—or not shared—guilt and triumph, in a way unprecedented even in that ecclesially tormented land. It is quite clear from Leuenberg itself and from the dialogues that led up to Leuenberg that without this terrible event, that sheer experience of fellowship which enabled Leuenberg would not have been possible. It is equally clear that this experience is not shared by American Reformed and Lutheran Christianity. That is not to say we cannot learn or have not learned much from the *Kirchenkampf*, only that it cannot for us supply the place of theological dialogue as it has on the continent.

Second, it is inescapable as one follows the trail of documents and commentary that the unargued unity that the partners experienced was in large measure given by joint opposition to Rome. At every step Marc Lienhard's remark applies, that throughout the discussions it seemed "as if our historical unity were best shown in opposition to Rome."[4] It is noteworthy that the matters not taken up in Leuenberg are exactly those important in conversation with Roman Catholicism: ecclesiology and the understanding of the ministry. The proposed outline of the Agreement contained sections on the church and on the ecclesial office; both were deliberately stricken.

LEUENBERG AND THE UNITED STATES: TWO DIFFERENT HISTORIES

Here again Leuenberg is enabled by a history that is very different from ours. Two differences are decisive.

First, there is a strange way in which Europe is confessionally more truly pluralistic than is the United States. From the foundation of modern Europe, three confessions have fought over and shared the spiritual definition of the continent. There have of course been Catholic territories and Evangelical territories; but especially so in the German-speaking heartland of Leuenberg. Moreover, after the war the German populations were shuffled.

In the United States, quite differently, two of the European confessions, Roman Catholicism and Lutheranism, made their significant entry on the scene late, into a world already religiously defined by the third, the Reformed. The founding of the seminary where I teach is a classic instance: Samuel Simon Schmucker was a graduate of Princeton Seminary and invented the American Lutheran seminary by deliberate imitation of Princeton. Calvinism has borne the burden of American culture-religion, Lutheranism and Roman Catholicism have not. Thus the way in which the three confessions have severally participated in the shaping experiences of American religious history is utterly different from the way in which they have participated in the shaping experiences of European religious history.

Second, in each case of Europe and America, there is one confession over against which the other two inevitably define themselves. But it is not the same one. In Europe, the very landscape daily reminds of pre-Reformation Christendom and of the great historical event that divided it. The Roman Catholic Church inescapably is experienced as the continuing representative of pre-Reformation Christendom, and the other two confessions as together the representatives of the Reformation.

The United States, very differently, had no part in pre-Reformation Christendom, or in the Reformation itself. Here it is Calvinist Christianity over against which other groups have jointly understood themselves. If Reformed and Lutheran in Europe instinctively understand themselves as *non-Catholic*, Catholics and Lutherans in the United States have both lived as outsiders and assimilees over against *Calvinism*.

Three consequences seem to me to follow from these observations. The first is the same as that which follows from the earlier set of observations: the history which in Europe substitutes for theological consensus cannot do so here, since it is not our history.

The second is that American Reformed Christianity has been transformed by the American experience in a way Lutheranism and Catholicism are only beginning to be. Whether, from an ecumenical point of view, this transformation has been for the better or the worse, need not concern us now. What is inescapable is that Lutheranism has in this country a very different partner, under the label "Reformed," than is signatory to Leuenberg.

The third consequence introduces a new topic.

ROBERT JENSON

LEUENBERG: AN AGREEMENT TO STAND AGAINST ROME?

For Lutheranism in America to adhere to Leuenberg—whether in itself or as the subtext of *An Invitation to Action*—would be an ecumenical choice of a sort which it perhaps was not in Europe: a deliberate move into an alliance over against Roman Catholicism. At least on this continent, where the natural commonalities do not fall as they do in Europe, it must be determinitative for any Lutheran use of Leuenberg, that precisely those questions that by Roman Catholic judgment continue to divide Roman Catholics and Lutherans—the nature of the church, the nature of ecclesial office, Eucharistic sacrifice—are defined by Leuenberg as incapable of dividing the church.

Also in Europe this point has not gone unnoticed. I cite André Birmelé: "The most important relevance . . . for the dialogue with Rome lies in a silence of the Leuenberg Agreement. . . . The understanding of the church and of its ministries has been postponed to the theological dialogues which accompany realized ecclesial communion. Leuenberg has been able to declare ecclesial fellowship without debating these questions. Such a tactic is inconceivable for the Roman Catholic church, for which an understanding of the church is inseparable from a consensus in the understanding of the gospel."[5]

But are not the Roman Catholics *right* in this last matter? Is not consensus in the understanding of the Church a necessary part of consensus in the understanding of the gospel? Or, anyway, do Lutherans in this country want to say that Leuenberg is right and Rome wrong, without further discussion of the enormous ecumenical choice thereby made? Unity is, after all, creedally confessed by Lutherans as an essential attribute of the church, and it is not unity of opinion about sacraments but unity in sacramental fellowship that the Augustana declares "*satis*."

Perhaps Lutherans on this continent will not wish to make the establishing of a common front against Rome the basis of a declaration of fellowship with our Reformed sisters and brothers. The question is anyway not about plots—whether there are such or no—but about the objective parameters of the choices to be made.

And indeed, some Europeans have made this choice in full consciousness, and press its consequences on every ecumenical occasion. So, for a particularly energetic example, Hans Grass attacked the joint Roman Catholic–Lutheran dialogue report on The Lord's Supper precisely so: In this document, there is too much "element-piety" and too much about "sacrifice," which is offensive precisely because it "threatens Leuenberg." "The understanding of real presence represented in this paper deviates from the line which was achieved in the Arnoldshain Theses and in the Leuenberg Concord."[6]

Nor has this possible character of the Leuenberg consensus gone unnoticed by Roman Catholics. We may hear an early Roman Catholic critic: "The decisive question about the proposed document (is) . . . the relationship to the Roman Catholic Church . . . One must call this question decisive, since the original and continuing target of all that is specifically reformatory is, after all, the Roman Catholic Church. Now, a . . . confession is only ecumenical . . . when it takes the partner seriously in its opposition. Precisely because we Catholic Christians affirm Luther's charismatic call to the gospel with radical seriousness, . . . we have the right to expect that our own position will be conscientiously tested by our partner. That does not happen here . . . In general, the ecumenical perspective is missing . . ."[7]

A FAILURE TO REACH CONSENSUS

Finally, we must ask whether in fact the one great matter with which Leuenberg does deal, the ancient and deeply theological and spiritual division over the Lord's Supper, does in fact find satisfactory consensus.

Even to discuss this, we must from the start be clear that *An Invitation to Action* utterly misuses Leuenberg, in the way in which it tries to make Leuenberg the basis of fellowship in America. As Marc Leinhard makes clear, Leuenberg's point was *not* to discover that the condemnations of the 16th century were based on misunderstanding, or are unimportant (which is precisely what the American documents assert); the question asked in Leuenberg was whether those condemnations hit the teaching of the actual churches now proposed to be taken into membership.[8] *An Invitation to Action*, unfortunately, did not even pose this question about the actual churches it proposes to bring into fellowship.

The Problem of the Eucharistic Presence

But now to the matter. Throughout the negotiations that led to Leuenberg and in the Agreement itself, the great alleged advance and the key which enabled Reformed and Lutherans to overcome their old quarrel about Christ's presence in the Eucharist, was that the "real presence was . . . not grasped in a static or physical manner; 'body' and 'blood' designate the person of Jesus Christ. . . . The accord is not established by agreement in any certain mode of Christ's presence by the bread and wine but in an understanding of what happens during the celebration of the Supper. The real presence is grasped in a dynamic and actualist fashion."[9] The goal and result was "a rejection of element- and consecration-piety" in that the "myth of locality" is overcome, whether this is the Lutheran "localization of the sacramental gifts in the elements" or the Calvinist localization of Christ's body in heaven.[10]

It is assuredly the case that understanding of Christ's Eucharistic presence must be understanding of his *personal* presence; and in my own teaching I have concentrated monomaniacally on just such understanding. But precisely therein, I have tried to break through to understanding of the *embodiment* of personal presence, to understanding of Christ's presence precisely as *this* body, the loaf and cup, and to understanding of the foundational position of this presence as the elements for Christ's specific presence at the Supper. It is not at all clear that in every discourse about "personal" and "dynamic" presence, "person" in fact means the same as "body and blood" in the narratives of institution. It is assuredly not clear that it means the same in Leuenberg.

The antithetical Reformed and Lutheran christological-sacramental positions expressed irreconcileable and profound interpretations of the whole of reality, which, in my judgment, have not been synthesized or transcended in Leuenberg. Over what was in fact at issue, Leuenberg contains no consensus at all; or if it does, it contains a consensus obtained by abandoning the Lutheran concern.

Nor is the consensus—or surrender, whichever it is—manifest only in the text on the Supper. We may compare what the final draft and the approved text say about baptism. In response to Lutheran complaint, reference to water is added while what it accomplishes in the name of the Father, Son, and Holy Spirit is muted.

I can do no better in this matter than to cite a recently deceased friend:

"Doubtless it was at first . . . a clarification, that we learned better to articulate the personalist and word-carried relations of faith. . . . But now . . . the quarrel of the Reformation has reappeared on this new level of understanding. . . . A spiritualising personalism [has appeared, which] in the dimension of the *coram Deo* flees from bodily-communicative concretion. . . . We are just willing to celebrate the Supper, and here we venture even so far as to take seriously the acts of eating and drinking, but from the earthly elements that are eaten and drunk we keep Christ's presence as distant as possible; we will just allow 'with,' but not 'in' or 'under,' and surely nothing like a *'praedicatio identica'* between the risen Lord and a created gift."[11]

It is not my view that the profound difference that obtains between Reformed and Lutheran understandings of Christ's presence is necessarily church-divisive. Indeed, I am one of those ecumenicists who is almost always hard put to discover any church-divisive differences at all. But we must not pretend that what is not solved has been, or base churchly fellowship on documents that make such pretense.

ROBERT JENSON

Notes

1. André Birmelé, *Le Salut en Jesus Christ, dans les dialogue occumenique* (Paris: Edition du Cerf, 1986), 212. (Hereafter cited as *Le Salut*.)
2. James E. Andrews and Joseph A. Burgess, eds., *An Invitation to Action: The Lutheran–Reformed Dialogue,* Series 3, 1981-1983 (Philadelphia: Fortress Press, 1984).
3. Marc Lienhard, *Lutherisch–Reformierte Kirchengemeinschaft Heute* (Frankfurt: Otto Lembeck, 1972), 32.
4. *Ibid.,* 71.
5. Birmelé, *Le Salut*, 420.
6. Hans Grass, "Die gemeinsame katholisch-lutherische Erklarung zum Herrenmahl," *Materialdienst des konfessionskundlichen Instituts Bensheim* 30 (1975): 87-92.
7. Albert Bandenburg, "Der Leuenberger Konkordienentwurf in der Sicht eines katholischen Teologens," in *Leuenberg—Konkordie oder Diskordie?* ed. Ulrich Asendorf and F. W. Kuenneth (Berlin: Die Spur, 1974), 169.
8. Marc Lienhard, "Die Verwerfungen die Irrlehre und das Verhaltnis zwischen lutherischen und reformierten Kirchen," in *Auf Dem Weg 2* (Zurich, 1971).
9. Birmelé, *Le Salut*, 410f.
10. Hans Grass, "Diskussionseinleitung," in *Wort und Abendmahl*, ed. R. R. Williams (Stuttgart: Evang. Missionsverlag, 1967), 22.
11. Albrecht Peters, "Unionistisches Mittelmas," in *Von der wharen Einheit der Kirche* (Berlin: Die Spur, 1973), 153.

8

Ecumenical Perspectives on the Leuenberg Agreement

Whenever churches set out to deepen their fellowship with other churches, all churches have reason to rejoice. I would like to place at the beginning of my reflections this joy and thankfulness for the ecumenical efforts of Lutheran, Reformed, and Union churches and ask that the following questions be understood in relation to these preliminary remarks.

In relation to the Leuenberg Agreement, I do not see the initial task of the Roman Catholic Church in evaluating from its own viewpoint the origin, methods, and text of Leuenberg. Rather, the Catholic church should first identify the ecumenical process of the Reformation churches, carefully attend to the its unfolding, and seek to understand its significance for the entire *oikumené*.

LEUENBERG AND NON-REFORMATION CHURCHES

Significant Aspects of the Agreement

The Agreement takes seriously the unity given to us in Jesus Christ. The separation of the churches creates a breach in the visible form of the body of Christ. Ecumenism is the search for forms of church life that will make visible our given unity. (This understanding became clear in the editing of the Agreement. In the outline of 1971, section 4 was titled "Establishment of Church Fellowship." In the final text of 1973, it was titled "Declaration of Church Fellowship.")

The Agreement had its origins in dialogues among Lutheran and Reformed theologians who could not have known that they were beginning a process that would lead to church fellowship among almost all the Reformation churches in Europe. It thus grew out of a lived ecumenism that impelled the churches along this path. A kind of *kairos* exists in the search for unity, a search which lives on "signs of the times" and cannot ignore them.

But concerns also arise here. There is perhaps a certain haphazardness, for example, in the choice of themes. Many of the themes of the first two series of dialogues at Arnoldshain and Schauenburg appear only on the periphery of Leuenberg. There also is a certain unevenness to events since Leuenberg. Not all participating churches experience the same urgency in the process. Criticism and rejection of the Agreement still exists, raising a concern for the unity of the participating churches. Ecumenical efforts must not lead to new divisions.

The Newness of Leuenberg

A change in method appears to me to distinguish the dialogues at Arnoldshain and Schauenburg from those at Leuenberg. The two earlier series still took as their basis the traditional controversial questions. At Leuenberg, however, the question was: what is the "center" of our common faith? What can we together affirm that can be the basis of church fellowship? In this change appears what I think is essentially new in the Leuenberg Agreement. Its "method" becomes a question for the ecumenical efforts of all churches. Seen from this center of a common faith, our differences take on an altered significance.

But again, concerns arise here: over the criteria that distinguish differences that are church-dividing from differences that can exist within church fellowship; and over the relative importance of the confessional texts and the text of the Agreement.

Leuenberg's "way to the center" seems to meet these concerns by giving church fellowship a "process" character consistent with its origin. The Agreement both specifies a result, the description of a common "center," and also initiates a fellowship committed to the task of discussing the remaining differences on the basis of this newly discovered commonality. The relation between commonality and difference must be constantly reexamined. The indispensable common center cannot be described once and for all. It can be further developed. But also the remaining differences can take on a character that disrupts this center. The "continuing doctrinal discussions" called for by the Agreement (37) thus have a special significance for the fellowship of the churches. The obligation to place these discussions in the "wider context" (49) of churches of other confessions shows the openness of Leuenberg toward a larger unity. Especially here the non-Reformation churches see the ecumenical character of the Agreement. The question arises, however, how these doctrinal dialogues can be given a form and a binding character which will correspond to their importance for the fellowship of the Reformation churches and for the total *oikumené*.

LEUENBERG AND ROMAN CATHOLIC THOUGHT

After these more personal remarks about aspects of the Agreement that seem to me important for the total *oikumené*, I would like to say something from a Roman Catholic perspective.

I must first note that there exists no official Roman Catholic response to the Agreement. Positively this is a function of a reticence regarding the union attempts of other churches. More negatively, however, ecumenical developments among other churches still receive little attention in the Roman Catholic Church.

Vatican II and Ecumenism

There are strands in the development of Roman Catholic theology that can be placed in close relation to the efforts of the

Agreement. The recognition of other Christian churches as communities of Jesus Christ by the Second Vatican Council Decree on Ecumenism gives the unity efforts of these churches a different relative importance for the Roman Catholic Church. In addition to this, Roman Catholic ecumenism since Vatican II has ceased to be an "ecumenism of return" which seeks only to reestablish an earlier form of "unity." Engagement with the Reformation has become an engagement with its criticism of the Roman church. Dialogues with the Reformation churches do more than work through doctrinal differences. They also address the "cleansing" of the Roman Catholic side from the one-sideness and distortion produced by the events of the Reformation and hardened by centuries of controversy. This process within Roman Catholic thought can only profit from the development of the Reformation churches and their doctrine.

It is especially noteworthy that the distinction between matters that belong to the "center" of church fellowship and matters that allow for diversity finds a parallel in the concept of the "hierarchy of truths" developed by Vatican II:

> Catholic theologians engaged in ecumenical dialogue, while standing fast by the teaching of the Church and searching together with separated brethren into the divine mysteries, should act with love for truth, with charity, and with humility. When comparing doctrines, they should remember that in Catholic teaching there exists an order of "hierarchy" of truths, since they vary in their relationship to the foundation of the Christian faith. Thus the way will be opened for this kind of fraternal rivalry to incite all to a deeper realization and a clearer expression of the unfathomable riches of Christ. (Decree on Ecumenism 14)

Some Roman Catholic Comments about the Agreement

From the comments of some Roman Catholic theologians directly about the Leuenberg Agreement, I wish to note some main points.

There is no doubt that the movement together of the Reformation churches creates anxiety in the Roman Catholic Church. The problem of the formation of church "blocks" was discussed by the churches at Leuenberg and has been perceived also from the Roman Catholic side. It seems easier to reach an understanding with individual churches than with the larger structure of a community of churches. (My personal judgment on this question has already been made clear; I think that the Roman Catholic Church can only profit from progress by the Reformation churches.)

Questions are raised about the range of churches that have joined in this Agreement. It is asked whether the Reformation is understood simply in terms of an opposition to Roman Catholicism and whether the search for unity must work from this presupposition. Something true is contained in this question. The relation among the Reformation churches is not simply a matter of their "battle" against Rome. It seems to me legitimate and necessary to explore the causes of the division among the Reformation churches and to test their differences in the context of contemporary theology.

A question *for me* is whether the orientation of the Leuenberg church fellowship toward article 7 of the Augsburg Confession can represent a stumbling block within the wider *oikumené*. In relation to other questions, the biblical witness consistently has been referred to. Can the limitation to the typical Reformation criteria be biblically broadened?

Comments on individual aspects of the Leuenberg Agreement focus consistently on four themes. First, from the perspective of the Roman Catholic understanding of the Church, one cannot concur with the reference to "office and ordination" as just one item in a list of topics for future doctrinal discussions (39). Second, the description of the gospel in terms of the doctrine of justification (6-12) is considered insufficient in light of the biblical witness. Third, the assertion of the real presence of Christ in the Lord's Supper within the formulation of the Agreement (15) is also considered insufficient. In particular, it lags behind that which has already been asserted in the Lutheran–Roman Catholic dialogue. Finally, it is asked whether it is appropriate that the sacrament of penance and the possibility of absolution go totally unmentioned. The Leuenberg Agreement is not the result of dialogues between the Roman Catholic and the Reformation churches. If in the future, however, the statements of the Leuenberg Agreement are to serve as a basis for a broader dialogue, then these questions will certainly need to be the first addressed.

I must mention one other contribution of Leuenberg that has become, in my judgment, extremely important for the Roman Catholic Church in recent years. This is the assessment in the present context of the doctrinal condemnations from the period of the Reformation.[1] The results of this assessment have recently been published. The impetus given by the Leuenberg Agreement to this assessment has been made clear in its Foreword and the accompanying official letters. On the basis of this experience, the existing doctrinal condemnations were taken up so that they might be examined and their church-dividing character tested. Lifting the condemnations does not mean that they simply have no further significance. Rather, it means that they do not today apply to the partner church. In this manner the way can also be made clear for common formulations by the Roman Catholic and Reformation churches.

DEVELOPMENTS SINCE 1973

In conclusion, I would like to mention five aspects that in my judgment are present in the Agreement and that have become significant in the years since its adoption.

Leuenberg wished to avoid the formation of a "Reformation block" and to take seriously the existing ecumenical relations of the individual churches. Each church has continued its own bilateral dialogues and at times has achieved far-reaching results. An example is the Lutheran–Roman Catholic dialogue here in the U.S. New ecumenical efforts and ecumenical results already achieved must not call each other into question; church fellowship is always stamped by the ecumenical strength of the individual churches and the forms they have discovered. In these bilateral dialogues, however, the question again arises of the relative significance of the Leuenberg Agreement. To what degree do the churches of the Agreement proceed on the basis of text and to what degree on the basis of their confessions?

The significance of the Agreement would be strengthened if it were used more often as the starting point for further dialogues. Leuenberg also did not seek to impose "uniformity" on the churches. Discussions of the meaning of "confessional identity" have again become lively in recent years. Positively, this development could mean that the different confessional styles in church life, worship, and hymnody have found their place as expressions of diversity within lived fellowship (see LA 28). Negatively, it could mean a retreat to one's own position, an obstruction of truly lived fellowship, and the frustration of the processes that I have described as the essential mark of church fellowship according to Leuenberg. The discussion of "confessional identity" will have to be pursued even more intensively.

In the process of investigating the causes of church division, Leuenberg found that "non-theological factors" were significant. Investigation of these non-theological factors needs to continue. In this connection we must ask whether new divisions are arising today which transcend confessional boundaries. These factors, perhaps long unnoticed, could lead to new divergences: for example, over the question of political action.

Working on the basis of the Arnoldshain and Schauenburg dialogues, Leuenberg described the confessional opposition in terms of the old controversial theological questions. We need to ask, however, whether the confessional opposition is removed when these controversies are cleared up. The experience of church fellowship will test whether new differences have developed in the centuries of separation which are now more pronounced than those deriving from the sixteenth century.

Finally, in recent years the need for a common witness of the churches to the burning questions of our time has accentuated the scandal of division. In the protection of creation and the pursuit of peace and justice in the world, we can find lines of connection among the churches that are independent of doctrinal differences. The urgency that impels our common Christian witness in this world can make us bold to face the differences that still exist among us, to clarify them further, and to give them the relative importance they deserve. Unity in the midst of living diversity will then become an image of the presence of God among humanity.

Notes

1. *The Condemnations of the Reformation Era: Do They Still Divide?*, ed. Karl Lehmann and Wolfhart Pannenberg, trans. Margaret Kohl (Minneapolis: Fortress Press, 1989).

G E R A L D   M O E D E

W I L L I A M   N O R G R E N

G E O R G E   T A V A R D

9

Observations by Other Lutheran Dialogue Partners

GERALD MOEDE

Your invitation to attend this consultation and to participate in this panel is very much appreciated. My observations need to be understood from the context in which I have worked for the past twenty-one years: the Faith and Order staff of the World Council of Churches (WCC), during the time that *Baptism, Eucharist and Ministry (BEM)* was being written; and as the general secretary of the Consultation on Church Union (COCU) for fourteen years, during the time a theological agreement was completed and sent to the churches for their assent, and a second form of unity called "covenanting" was developed. Thus I trust that what I say will not be presumptuous, touching as it does some dimensions of unity that have not occupied you thus far in this consultation.

I wish first to comment on the matter of context. It has been suggested here that the national or regional context is important, even vital. And, in my opinion, there is much truth to that assertion. In COCU, for example, we see that the national context is critical. Unity needs to be manifested on the national level because unity in each place is important, and the national "place" is one that should not be ignored. There is a certain uniqueness to each national expression of unity that needs to be considered. And this uniqueness of place extends to the "local place" as well.

Raymond George, an English Methodist leader, once asked what the value was of his being in communion with another Methodist in Latin America whom he scarcely saw if he was not in communion with the Presbyterian down the street whom he could scarcely avoid.

A shared context is important; shared experience, or a shared crisis (like that of the European churches after the Second World War) has helped shape readiness in more than one "union" conversation since 1925, helping to prepare a particular *kairos*. One can demonstrate the importance of shared experience in a variety of places, such as Canada in their union of 1925, India in 1947, and Australia in the '70s.

If I have understood, however, it has been suggested here that such shared perspective was the *only* reason for agreement being reached in the Leuenberg conversation, and that therefore agreements arising in it would not be applicable elsewhere. But if that is so, would not the international bilateral agreements be invalidated, as well as the agreement of the Faith and Order Commission?

In the Consultation on Church Union, which has taken the national context very seriously, we have certainly been influenced and aided by agreements that had previously been reached in other contexts, such as the Church of South India and *BEM*. In these cases, a similar context was not shared, but the agreement reached in one place was applicable in another. Might that not be the case with the Leuenberg Agreement as well?

The "adequacy" of the Leuenberg Agreement for the American mileau has also been questioned. It is certainly true that in different places, the argumentation might seem sparse and terse. But it might also be that shared crisis has a way of clearing the mind, of getting to the real basics. And a multi-church effort such as Leuenberg just might find that it could state old problems and suggest different solutions in new ways, and that as trust in one another grew, there could even be toleration of some unexplained mystery! Furthermore, Professor Jenson may certainly express doubt as to whether the Leuenberg agreement would be adequate in the American context. But I become uneasy when (if I understood him correctly) he seems to cast doubt as to whether it should have been adequate in its own context.

There is a second question I would raise: the place and influence of *BEM*. Does that significant document, developed over fifty years with the theologians of more than 100 churches taking part, have a role to play in your situation? This is simply to suggest that multilateral dialogues are really identifying new categories that can help lead us beyond some of the old impasses. Remember how this past summer, the meeting of Anglican bishops at Lambeth articulated unprecedented appreciation for *BEM*. Within this question another might emerge: Would it not be important and helpful for your Roman Catholic and Reformed conversations to be in very close touch with one another? They might well influence each other in a positive manner. In the United Methodist–Lutheran bilateral on episcopacy, for example, the United Methodist bishops' response to *BEM* was helpful in bringing some new thinking to traditional Methodist positions on the place and ministry of the bishop.

Third question, that of timing. From our experience, it would seem valuable to plan for your Roman Catholic and Reformed dialogue to take place simultaneously so that "cross-pollination" might take place. This has certainly happened in a valuable way in the theological work of the Consultation on Church Union, where a working consensus has developed and has been accepted now by seven churches as an "adequate expression, in the matters with which it deals, of the apostolic faith." Within this larger effort, there have been two traditional church unions. Each has influenced the others. But each has been influenced as well by the "catholic" dimension of the overarching conversation.

Fourth is the question of "mission." We remember that mission was one of the basic factors behind the birth and development of the ecumenical movement. What place should it play in your developing conversations? This is not only an academic concern. For example, Bishop Lesslie Newbigin reminds us, from both a Catholic and Protestant perspective, that regular inter-communion without regular shared mission is a "profaning of the sacrament." The goal of our theological discussion is not only unity for its own sake, but also shared life in the world.

And finally, the question of how we *do* theology. In a sense, this relates back to my first question—context. In COCU we have been forced, primarily by the predominantly Black churches, to hear, consider, and incorporate various theological viewpoints into our proposed agreement, including elements of so-called liberation theology. We have intentionally sought the theological contributions of Black and feminist Christians. This means, first of all, the *presence* of such persons in the commissions that do this work.

The responses already received in Geneva to *BEM* make it clear that those coming from the so-called third world are not as concerned about some of the traditional "Faith and Order" questions as are those of us from the first and second worlds. These third world Christians are about to attain numerical superiority of the total Christian community. What do they have to teach us?

Those who participated in this consultation sang with enthusiasm and devotion one of Charles Wesley's great hymns, in which the matter of sanctification or perfection was held up. Are you open to such viewpoints as you do theology in the future? Is there more than one acceptable way to do theology? Involved in this question, of course, is the deeper issue of catholicity.

Perhaps the basic question then is this: If mission imperatives have brought us to a new awareness of the biblical imperative to manifest unity, may we assume that the Holy Spirit can and will lead us to understand and bridge old disagreements in new and even different ways? How we answer that question is crucial.

WILLIAM NORGREN

As a Christian of the Anglican tradition, I wish to express my gratitude for your invitation. At the same time, I feel some ambiguity about being here because Anglicans in Europe were not involved in drafting the Leuenberg Agreement.

We agree and rejoice in those parts of the text that witness to the centrality of the gospel of Jesus Christ. I wonder, however, if the agreement does not focus the primary unity of the Lutheran and Reformed traditions in the Reformation events of the sixteenth century—or rather, in some of these events, for the Agreement is silent about other churches influenced by Reformation events. My question is, to what degree can it be said that "tradition alone"—the tradition of the Reformation—is the core of the agreement?

This echoes the question of the Schieffer paper: "whether the orientation of the Leuenberg church fellowship toward article 7 of the Augsburg Confession can represent a stumbling block within the wider *oikoumemé* . . . Can the limitation to the typical Reformation criteria be biblically broadened?" (See above, 111). In my understanding, such broadening needs to be directed particularly to the doctrine of the church and the church's ministry, both of which are inescapably implicated in the proclamation of the gospel and the administration of the sacraments. The Leuenberg Agreement suggests a separation.

In appealing for a wider horizon, I call attention again to the Schieffer paper. According to the author, "there exists no official Roman Catholic response to the [Leuenberg] Agreement. Positively this is a function of reticence regarding the union attempts of other churches. More negatively, however, ecumenical developments among other churches still receive little attention in the Roman Catholic church" (See above, 109). You could add "Anglican" or other churches to this comment. Perhaps this consultation will be the beginning of a wider evaluation and response to the agreement.

GEORGE TAVARD

I wish to express my appreciation, both for the opportunity to take part in this consultation and for the paper given by Professor Elisabeth Schieffer. My brief remarks will touch on some points that are raised in this paper.

First, it seems that there is a difference in mentality between North America and at least some parts of Europe in regard to Roman

Catholic reactions to the efforts to reach a closer unity among the churches issued from the continental Reformation. Dr. Schieffer writes: "There is no doubt" that such a move "creates an anxiety in the Roman Catholic church." Now, I am quite certain that Catholics in North America, and specifically the Catholic bishops, feel no such anxiety or even apprehension. On the contrary, it has been the constant policy of the Bishops' Commission for Ecumenical and Interreligious Affairs, since its creation in 1965, to regard all movements toward closer unity among Christian churches as a contribution to the ultimate reconciliation of all. No fear was expressed when the Consultation on Church Union started. And to my knowledge, the Canadian bishops did not express any anxiety when the United Church of Canada came into being. There would not be any more anxiety if the Lutheran churches were actively involved in these movements. The process of reunion among Protestant churches must keep its integrity, and the need for it to do so is respected by the Roman Catholic church in the USA. Such endeavors are regarded with Christian optimism and trust in the Holy Spirit, for the ecumenical movement is, and should remain, one.

Second, I would draw attention to the expression, "communities of Jesus Christ" (*Gemeinschaften Jesu Christi*), that is used by Dr. Schieffer. I take it that, in the paper, this expression translates the Latin formula of the decree on Ecumenism of Vatican Council II: *communitates ecclesiales*.[1] In the texts of Vatican II, it is clear that the Catholic church fully recognizes the ecclesial status of the Orthodox churches. It follows in this a long tradition. In regard to the churches issued from the Reformation, the Council uses a twofold expression, *ecclesiae et communitates ecclesiales*: "churches and ecclesial communities." One may of course wonder what an ecclesial community can be, if it is not a church! But there is a reason behind this double formula. It lies in the approach adopted by the Council toward the visibility of the church. In the Catholic tradition, the church is closely tied to the Eucharist.[2] When they gather together, the faithful are constituted as the church by the Eucharist that they share. Therefore the Council does not start from the church to acknowledge the Eucharist. Rather, it starts from the Eucharist to recognize the church. Where it finds the Eucharist, it finds the church. The more a Christian community is committed to the Eucharist, the clearer therefore will be its ecclesial status in the eyes of the Roman Catholic church. But it was not the task of the Council to decide which among the churches of the Reformation can thus be recognized as being gathered around the Eucharist. Hence the formula it used, which opens the way to ecumenical exchanges concerning the importance of the Sacrament. Third, this approach ought to be related to the basic understanding of the church. The Reformation focused attention on two marks, notes, or signs, of the church: "where the Word is preached and the sacraments are administered according to the gospel." This was in fact an amplification of the definition of the church by Thomas Aquinas: The church is the gathering of the faithful (*congregatio fidelium*). Aquinas, and medieval theology in general, did not define the church by the hierarchy or *magisterium*. This is a later point of view, typical of the Counter-Reformation, for which Cardinal Bellarmine, who was a Jesuit (not by accident!), was chiefly responsible. Defining the church by the faithful, one implicitly raises the question, what makes the faithful to be faithful? They are faithful because they have heard the Word of God in the Holy Spirit, and they have been led by it to Christ, present among us in the Eucharist. Thus, the church's self-realization rests upon the Word and the sacraments, central to which is the Eucharist. This is in fact close to the fundamental understanding of the church at Vatican Council II. It is apparent today that the underlying ecclesiology of the conciliar documents is not the notion of the people of God, or that of the mystical body, though both are clearly formulated. The fundamental ecclesiology is that the church is the communion of the faithful, gathered in Christ through the Holy Spirit. *Communio* or *koinonia* is the basic category. This ecclesiology has immediate ecumenical implications.The *Final Report* of ARCIC-I (1983)[3] pointed this out when it declared that its agreed statements were based on a *communio*-ecclesiology. In several addresses, Cardinal Willebrands has drawn the ecumenical implications of this ecclesiology: the universal church can only be a Communion between churches that follow different *typoi*, a *typos* being the totality of the liturgies, forms of prayer, theologies, formulations, customs, confessions of faith, of a given church.[4] Each such *typos* must be respected in the communion of the whole. More recently, the French theologian, Jean-Marie Tillard, has extensively analyzed this communion of communions.[5] Precisely, there is a convergence between this conciliar accent and the ecclesiology that is suggested in the Leuenberg Agreement: "Church fellowship means that . . . churches with different confessional positions accord each other fellowship in word and sacrament (29).

In conclusion, far from being unwelcome to Catholics, or sensed by them as a threat to catholicity, the Leuenberg Agreement contributes to the ecclesiology of *communio* that has been one of the most promising fruits of Vatican Council II.

Notes

1. *Vatican Council II: The Conciliar and Post Conciliar Documents, Vol. 2*, ed. Austin Flannery (Leaminster, England: Fowler Wright Book, 1981), 252.
2. *Ibid.*, "Dogmatic Constitution on the Church," 350ff.
3. *Growth in Agreement*, ed. Meyer, Harding, and Vischer (New York: Paulist Press; Geneva: World Council of Churches), 61.
4. Note the address given by Cardinal Willebrands at the Great St. Mary's Church, Cambridge, England, on January 18, 1970. It is published in *Called to Full Unity: Documents on Anglican–Roman Catholic Relations, 1966–1983*, ed. J. Witmer and R. Wright (U.S.C.C. Publication, 1985), 45-53.
5. Jean-Marie Tillard, *Eglise d'Eglices. L'ecclesiologie de communion* (Paris: Le Cerf, 1984).

10

Summary Observations

KARLFRIED FROELICH

I suspect that I was asked to share some final reflections with you because I am a member of the Lutheran team in the new round of Reformed-Lutheran conversations in this country. Most of you are aware that this group, which has just resumed its work, is still wrestling with the problem of its proper agenda. Where do we start? How much can be presupposed? What are the remaining issues between us? Where do we go from here? These questions are not as innocent as they appear at first glance. They carry the freight of history: not only a history that goes back to the sixteenth century, but also of the history of very recent years with their enthusiasm, their achievements, their hopes, their failures, their disappointments, and their pain.

To us team members, this consultation perhaps has been as bewildering as it was helpful. We have picked up during these days many suggestions, official and unofficial, explicit and implicit. Sign

123

Leuenberg! Modify Leuenberg! Forget Leuenberg! Endorse *An Invitation to Action*! Rewrite *An Invitation to Action*! Work on specific theological topics! Do not get bogged down in hairsplitting theological controversy! There were also lucid signals of the central point. The review of Leuenberg reminded all of us with unmistakable urgency that the goal must be the advance of *Kirchengemeinschaft*, nothing less. From the discussions at this consultation it has become clear that a great deal of real sharing between the churches is going on already. Personal and communal ties between Lutheran and Reformed Christians are as strong as they have been for some time in Europe and elsewhere. Serious dialogue has taken place and has produced palpable results in the form of published statements and study materials. Official actions by Reformed and Lutheran church bodies are already a matter of public record. All of this adds up to an impressive reality which cannot be ignored.

It is my conviction that the new round of conversations between the ELCA and its Reformed sister churches cannot come up with anything less. The task is one of completion, not of reconsideration. Thus, I regard our conversations as a new opportunity, the gift of a new *kairos* in the biblical sense of the word. *Kairos* means God's time, the opportunity of the right moment challenging us to embrace it. We are human. Our churches are human. Their pilgrimage, just as our own, is marked by unused *kairoi*, missed opportunities. What can we do once a *kairos* has been missed? Complaining, accusing, resigning, or giving up is not the Christian answer. We must take seriously the reality of forgiveness and new beginnings which is at the heart of our common Reformation heritage as Leuenberg has spelled it out again. It places justification in the center, and that means justification of the sinner, of vulnerable, fallible churches which do not always live up to the challenge of God's *kairos*. We all live by forgiveness, and this should encourage us to go at it again.

Quite specifically, I think I have learned some important lessons from our discussion of Leuenberg. I see again the importance of *context*. The Leuenberg Agreement emerged in its own specific context, the context of the life of particular churches in a particular corner of the world. The context in the United States is different.

And yet, the text has its own claim to make as a bold and confident declaration of commonness in the faith of the Reformation. Texts are exportable; they can go out and create their own context elsewhere, as the story of the Lutheran confessions in this country and the inclusion of the Barmen Declaration in the Presbyterian *Book of Confessions* (1967) demonstrate. They are exportable inasmuch as, despite their contextual limitations, they reflect the common center.

I have also learned about the importance of *process*. As we heard, the Leuenberg Agreement was not just the result of a process; its adoption by the churches was the central event in the ongoing process of reception and ownership. Things will not be different in this country. Our talks need to continue, but we will also need to look for central "confessional" events and statements, central marking points in our journey together. Most of all, we will have to begin living together more closely, more consciously, more ready for a common future. Before us is an immense educational task of encouraging our people on both sides to scrap old prejudice, to begin living together more intimately, more honestly, more trustingly as members of the same family, the same marriage if you will. A marriage only begins with the wedding. It *is* in its *becoming*, and this will need ongoing conversations over a long time, far beyond the declarations we are working toward. Nothing is worse than a marriage where there is nothing left to talk about any more.

GABRIEL FACKRE

I do not have a history in Lutheran–Reformed dialogue to match that of Karlfried Froelich; nevertheless, I am pleased to make some concluding comments. In my case, they reflect an association with the World Council of Churches and its address of similar themes.

My first impression has been of a stimulating, indeed energizing theological forum: The intra-Lutheran exchange between Jenson and Sundberg, Fries's forthright comments on Reformed restlessness, the intensity with which our European colleagues scrutinized the details of the Leuenberg Agreement. How many forehead veins are distended today by discussion of the hypostatic union or the *epiklesis*? Wonderful! Here is theological passion and substance—people caring about things worth caring about.

Of course there is another side to all this. The occupational hazard of theologians is "theological rabies." The foaming mouth can accompany the furrowed brow. I did not detect any symptoms of that disease here, but we would be naive not to be wary of it.

Impressions aside, I want to speak now about the substantive issues. First, Leuenberg. Second, the value of a Lutheran–Reformed conversation.

LEUENBERG

A key accent in Lienhard's paper and remarks had to do with Leuenberg's effort to get to "the heart of Scripture," "the core," "the common foundation," as a basis for church fellowship. I was struck by the determination to do this, in the light of today's widespread hermeneutical relativism. In academic theology it is regularly assumed that social location so shapes perception and communication that no common core is accessible; or that the power of vested interest so controls interpretation that what purports to be a common core is the disguised agenda of one or another partisan. A suspicionist hermeneutic scorns talk of "the heart of Scripture." The ecclesial result of this tends to be withdrawal into one's own hermeneutical bastion. And with it goes the ghettoization of theology and church life.

Conventional wisdom to the contrary notwithstanding, I join the Leuenbergers in the belief that there is a "common foundation," and that the quest for it is worth undertaking. We must resist the fashionable hermeneutical nihilism. And we have to do it collegially—in ecumenical conversation—for that is the corrective in this finite and fallen world for the things that do skew our perception. Further, I share the belief that the core has to do with the trinitarian history of God with its center in the person and justifying work of Christ, believed and lived in a eucharistic community in mission to the world. This is the common center (Schieffer) that binds us, one that has implications for the unity of the Church.

A second institutional observation is related to the impressive array of 80 national church bodies that are now part of the Agreement. The range of membership is enabled by carefully formulated language that speaks of commonality in "confessions *and* traditions." As a representative of the United Church of Christ, I took particular note of the "and." Given our church's mixed presbyterial and congregational polity, its corporate confessions are modest. But our "traditions" are inexorably active in the formation of who we are. Thus the above-noted common core is manifest more in our lectionary and liturgical life, our hymnody, our educational patterns and pastoral formation, our congregational and denominational ethos, piety and praxis (including a creedal and catechetical heritage) than in developed and universally agreed-upon doctrinal statements. As with the United Reformed Church in England and others, so with us, "confessions and traditions" constitute our theological identity.

LUTHERAN–REFORMED CONVERSATION

My principal observations have to do with the value of Lutheran–Reformed dialogue in the North American context.

It's tough going. One reason is the unresolved issues among Lutheran partners, as evidenced by the Jenson–Sundberg exchange. Related to that is the perceived impediment to Roman Catholic–Lutheran relations that seems to go with Lutheran–Reformed agreements. (However, the weakening or severing of the latter can also be read as a signal of diminished ecumenical relationships of another sort.)

In the light of these difficulties, there are moments when Reformed partners might be tempted to say: "Who needs this? Two more years of polarities and ambiguities? Could Reformed time be better spent in more productive conversations—with COCU? In other bilaterals? In the World Council of Churches project, "Toward a Common Expression of the Apostolic Faith"? Or, more to the point of Lutheran–Reformed possibilities, why not urge our churches simply to study and adopt the Leuenberg Agreement? By so doing, Reformed church-people in North America would enter into altar and pulpit fellowship with Lutherans around the world. And to these considerations, the UCC could add its own footnote: "We are already in pulpit and altar fellowship with Lutherans through our EKU–UCC agreement."

While the going *is* tough, however, I believe the effort is worth it. Engagement with the obstacles can work to the benefit of both Lutheran and Reformed constituencies. Questions posed by Lutherans to Reformed, and vice versa, force consideration of matters too easily neglected by each partner.

What the Reformed Need to Learn

Speaking of the Reformed tradition, I must say that our witness runs the risk of reductionism without the corrective from certain key accents in Lutheran theology and piety. To be in a conversation that brings us up sharply before our limitations and temptations can only do good things for us. Several cases in point:

An Achilles heel of the Reformed tradition is a simplistic accent on the divine sovereignty. We are eager to honor the holiness of God and affirm the divine majesty. How right that is: *non capax infiniti*! But an undialectical view of the divine freedom can distance God from the drudgery and toil of common things, so arise our vulnerabilities to a Nestorian Christology, sectarian ecclesiology, and Zwinglian sacramentology. Zeal to protect the divine majesty must be chastened by the truth in the Lutheran *capax infiniti*: God is not only free from, but is also free for us. The divine solidarity with us in Jesus Christ is God's "haveability" (Bonhoeffer). Reformed faith must not be content only with the language of "But . . ."; it must learn about the "*Yes*, but." That means strong commitment to Chalcedon's "without separation" (hypostatic union and the exchange of properties), the alien holiness of a Church made up of sinners as well as saints, the real presence in eucharistic action and elements, the ministry of Christ that continues in and through our frail ministries. All these things come hard to Reformed sensibilities.

For all our emphasis on the majesty of God, there is also in the Reformed tradition an ironic tendency too quickly to identity this or that cause with the divine purposes. Just because we want to honor that majesty by obedience, by the doing of God's will in the civil community and the hearing of God's Word in the Scripture, we are tempted to associate the glory of God with some human vessel or vehicle.

Thus Calvinist witness to the sovereignty of God over the public square easily turns into the divine endorsement of the movement, issue, cause we there advocate. Gone is the awareness of human frailty, as our legions of light contest their armies of darkness. Apocalyptic movements for social change—from the Christian right to Christian left—regularly march under Reformed banners (currently, the phalanxes of political fundamentalism, with the first ranks made up of the orthodox Calvinist Reconstructionists). We are reminded in Lutheran piety and theology about the sin even (and especially) in the righteous, and thus the ambiguity of our noblest causes. Reinhold Niebuhr, shaped by his Evangelical Synod heritage, taught a generation about these things; although his Reformed sensitivities (in that same Evangelical Church which brought together Lutheran and Reformed lineage) also struck that warning note of a divine sovereignty beyond our plans and purposes. Interestingly, Lutheran and Reformed traditions at their best can converge on this point as in the Barmen Declaration, co-drafted by a Barth and an Asmussen.

A Lutheran corrective to Reformed temptations is at work also in the interpretation of the Bible. It's a short step from a Calvinist reading of Scripture as co-extensive with Christ to a fundamentalist hermeneutic, as in the hard-line inerrancy among heirs of the Princeton school. Necessary is Luther's christological lens that distinguishes law from Gospel within Scripture.

What Lutherans Need to Learn

We need the Lutherans, and the Lutherans need us. Learning goes both ways. So Birmelé, on just the same issues spoken of here, rightly speaks of the "principle for complementarity."

Lutherans need the "Yes, *but*," the Reformed qualification. Solidarity cannot do without sovereignty. That means in Christology an attention to Chalcedon's "without confusion," and thus wariness about the seductions of Monophysitism. In ecclesiology this means the recognition that while the Church is, indeed, the Body of Christ, it is not the "continuation of the Incarnation." In sacramentology it points to the role of the Spirit in the eucharistic action. In the doctrine of ministry it means the recognition of collegiality in *episkope*, including the dispersion of the Spirit among the whole people of God (already implicit in Luther's priesthood of all believers). And all these things, the *capax* must learn to live with the *non capax*.

In ethics, Lutherans need to hear Reformed accents. God is the Sovereign to whom we are accountable in society as well as in the church and the soul. Indeed, the regency of Jesus Christ extends over the marketplace and the counting house. As such, the systems and structures of this world must answer to Christ's own rule, not to lesser or more accommodating norms (however much the implementation of those rigorous standards must take into account the fallen state of these powers and principalities, thus acknowledging that our best efforts are ambiguous and that our strategies must rightly be realistic—the Lutheran corrective in the best of two kingdom theory).

In hermeneutics, the Reformed espousal of the whole canon, however expressed—a multi-covenant theology, Old Testament as full partner with the New in theology, piety and politics, etc.—can remind Lutherans of the danger of a "canon within a canon" that precludes the surprises to be found at any place in the whole of Scripture, or the temptations of a Marcionite version of law and gospel juxtaposition. How much we need each other!

EVANGELICAL CATHOLICITY

My final observation is of a more personal nature, and has to do with the United Church of Christ. I believe that the ELCA in its present internal struggle for self-definition could profit from the

United Church of Christ experience. Our heritage includes a 150-year experiment in which our Mercersburg theologians, Nevin and Schaff spoke (first?) of "evangelical catholicity," and launched a movement to turn Reformation churches in that direction. There is a certain deja vu in reading appeals to the same in Lutheran journals. And a puzzlement too, when those appeals are made in conjunction with urgings to disconnect from the Reformed relationship in order to pursue more single-mindedly this evangelical catholic agenda.

As one of the founders of the present Mercersburg Society, with a ten-year history at the seminary of Nevin and Schaff (Lancaster Theological Seminary), I found many of the current issues in the ELCA anticipated in the early Mercersburg struggle. Nevin and Schaff attacked the Church's captivity to individualism, including Lutheran subjectivism as well as Reformed pietism; and called for catechetical integrity, sacramental objectivity and a high doctrine of the ministry. With it all went Nevin's much-discussed period of "dizziness"—a vertiginous attraction to an idealized Rome. Does all this sound familiar?

At its best (in the *Mercersburg Review*), evangelical catholicity took both words with absolute seriousness: "evangelical" as an unswerving commitment to the Reformation, "catholicity" as a refusal to overleap medieval and patristic epochs or to begin theological history at the sixteenth century. Evangelical catholicity, therefore, means inclusivity, a passion for the fullness of the gospel and rejection of the "sect mentality" whether that expressed itself in the "anxious bench" of pietism or the "sect mentality" of a Reformed, Lutheran, Congregational, or Roman Catholic exclusivism. It's no accident that Mercersburg laid the foundations for ecumenism in this country. And its contribution is manifest also in the formation of the United Church of Christ with its own embodiment of the complementarity of theological witness, and its commitment to inclusivity on issues of race, sex, class, and condition. We know something about both the difficulty and the directions of evangelical catholicity and are glad for those of kindred spirit.

Living with Mercersburg teaches one the need to render more explicit what is entailed in both the adjective "evangelical" and the noun "catholicity." The world-formative dimension of Christian faith could get lost in preoccupation with the evangelical soul or the catholic church. Thus the Geneva heritage is needed too—the stewardship of the life of the human city to divine purposes, setting up signs here to the city of God yet to be. So with the larger ecumenical movement, let us make it a threesome. The church penultimate that mirrors the church ultimate is a church "evangelical, catholic and reformed." A continuing conversation between two peoples—Lutheran and Reformed—could make its contribution to this larger end.

11

Reflections

MARY B. HAVENS

The consultation on the Leuenberg Agreement presented us with an abundance of food for thought, assessment, and reassessment. Perhaps it also has given many a new or renewed ecumenical vision: a way of seeking in integrity and authenticity to manifest the essential unity of Christ's church.

An integral aspect of that vision is remembrance of the roads already traveled, the work already accomplished. We can forget this past only at our own peril. Thankfully, graciously, we do not start *de novo*, but with the insights and the historical signposts of previous Lutheran–Reformed relations: the Wittenberg Concord, the Arnoldshain and the Schauenburg discussions, the Leuenberg Agreement, *Marburg Revisited*, and *An Invitation to Action*. It is the appreciation and ownership of this past that will save us from aimless amnesia. What we do in the new round of conversations must and will be cognizant of this past and in dialogue with it.

We have also heard and experienced how this past has given rise and encouragement to a hermeneutic of suspicion. There are wounds and scars—some not yet healed—from previous conversations. It is imperative that we acknowledge this reality and promote the necessary healing. Unlike many of our Reformed sisters and brothers, those of us appointed as Lutheran representatives to the conversation were not participants in earlier rounds of conversations. Many of us arrived here with varying degrees of knowledge and ignorance about the immediate past, especially that surrounding *An Invitation to Action*. We lost some of our innocence here. At times the experience was painful, but it was necessary; for we must know the historical truth in all its glories, frustrations, and failures. It is imperative that we know the totality of past endeavors in order to work faithfully and responsibly now, with our partners, in this task that has been entrusted to us by our respective churches. We cannot ignore the wounds of the veteran warriors or the retired generals of previous conversations, but must admit the pain and allow it expression; otherwise we will perpetually be the victim, and the hermeneutic of suspicion will haunt us in nightmarish ways. In allowing it expression, we can then proceed with the work to be done.

In offering critical analyses and interpretations of the Leuenberg Agreement, this consultation has opened vistas of theological, pastoral, contextual, and methodological considerations and possibilities. The candid opportunities for discussion and shared reflection have been of invaluable assistance in clarifying issues and providing pointers toward agenda formation. The formal and informal willingness to risk differing opinions, while sometimes uncomfortable, was invaluably stimulating; and even more crucial, it ensured an integrity which is essential to the process. In that, this consultation has achieved its desired objective, namely, the very process of dialogue such as it occurred here. So the conclusion of this consultation is but the beginning. We now begin the fourth round of Lutheran–Reformed conversations with the vision and the momentum to faithfully and responsibly converse with one another in a movement toward *Kirchengemeinschaft*, toward manifesting that unity already given in the Lord of the Church who prayed "that they may all be one" (John 17:21).

On behalf of the Lutheran partners in this conversation, I wish to express our appreciation to Drs. Rusch and Martensen, who so beautifully orchestrated the event. We are grateful also to Professors Lienhard, Birmelé, Meyer, and Schieffer, for their willingness to share their insights and experiences with the Leuenberg Concord. The seriousness with which Professors Fries, Sundberg, and Jenson approached their assignments has already borne much fruit and provided us with that critical insight and challenge we need. Thank you to all of you for the sacrifices you made to attend this consultation and your commitment to engage in the process. Now we begin our task. I am pleased to report that at our initial meeting there was a clear sense of commitment and mutual trust that will enable the process to continue. We do take seriously the complexity of our task and will engage in the necessary critical work required of us to fulfill that task with integrity and responsibility.

KEITH NICKLE

I am grateful that you included us, the participants in the recently organized Lutheran–Reformed conversations, as participants in this consultation. You did so persuaded that the Leuenberg experience could instruct us as we address our task. We have been instructed by the many stimulating exchanges. We have been moved by the seriousness with which issues critical to Lutheran and Reformed rapprochement here in the U.S. were addressed. And we have been encouraged by the enthusiasm with which you communicate the persuasion that positive progress in Lutheran–Reformed conversations really matters to the future shape of both our denominational traditions. We welcome that conviction and share it, convinced that in the extended history of Lutheran and Reformed interchanges here in the United States something very precious and very essential is at stake in terms of our growth in understanding of what it means to be the community of faith in these times.

Personally, I was greatly heartened by the consternation that surfaced across the board early on in this consultation at the recognition that Leuenberg could claim only "minimal concrete results" in "the search for a common commitment in the face of ethical, social and political challenges" ("Realizing Church Fellowship," by André Birmelé), in spite of the fact that the Leuenberg Agreement identified as a central goal of that agreement "the fullest possible cooperation in witness and service to the world" (29). To my mind, that is a major agenda item for the Leuenberg subscribers to pursue, for effective engagement of the community of faith with the world is the acid test for all such agreements. Any mutual recognition through ecumenical reception that we may orchestrate in the United States through the Lutheran–Reformed conversations or in any other way, but which does not compel us to intensify the ministry of the entire people of God in the arena of ethics and of social justice, squanders energies and resources that could and should be more faithfully invested elsewhere. Even assuming the successful conclusion of the conversations just now beginning, which would result in mutual ecumenical recognition and reception between our two ecclesiastical traditions, the task has only begun.

We in the Reformed family of Christian communities need the stimulus of full church fellowship with our Lutheran colleagues, so that they might compel us to get serious about the concrete implications for service inherent in the faith we preach and profess in common. We make bold to believe we can be of some similar help to Lutheran Christians. *An Invitation to Action* claimed "a common conviction of the urgency of God's mission confronting identical social, political, and cultural problems which require the united proclamation, witness and service of Christians."[1] That urgency, still there, *compels* us to get on with our conversations with all due, deliberate haste.

Renewal is not best pursued unilaterally in these days. Lasting, effective renewal is stimulated by affirmation and celebration of the solidarity with which we are gifted and enriched by God. It is that solidarity, that unity in Christ, which enables us, even empowers us, to incarnate in a persuasive way the presence of the merciful, liberating love of God to the poor, the blind, the captive, the oppressed.

I have found this consultation on the Leuenberg Agreement immensely rich and stimulating as a resource for Lutheran–Reformed conversations. It has invigorated our imaginations by raising questions, clarifying issues, and indicating pathways to be addressed and explored. We are grateful to the Strasbourg contingent for giving us greater access to the rich history leading up to Leuenberg, its considerable accomplishments, and the subsequent developments related to it. We are grateful for the presence and contribution of the other ecumenical delegates for broadening the scope of our engagement with Leuenberg's witness. And we are grateful to the Standing Committee on Ecumenical Affairs of the ELCA and its staff for mounting this consultation and for including us in its deliberations. We count it a signal learning experience.

We covet your continued good will and prayers as we address the task we have been assigned.

Notes

1. *An Invitation to Action: The Lutheran–Reformed Dialogue, Series 3, 1981-1983*, ed. James E. Andrews and Joseph A. Burgess (Philadelphia: Fortress Press, 1984), 4.

Appendix:
The Leuenberg Agreement

An Agreement, or Statement of Concord, between the Reformation churches of Europe was adopted by the Preparatory Assembly in completed form on March 16, 1973, in the Swiss conference center of Leuenberg. Intended to foster fellowship between the "Lutheran and Reformed churches in Europe along with the Union churches that grew out of them, and the related pre-Reformation churches, the Waldensian Church and the Church of the Czech Brethren" in terms of mutual recognition, the Leuenberg Agreement, as it has come to be called, has been transmitted to all involved European churches as well as to churches in other parts of the world.

Over the signatures of Dr. André Appel (Lutheran World Federation), Dr. Edmond Perret (World Alliance of Reformed Churches), and Dr. Lukas Vischer (Faith and Order Secretariat, World Council of Churches), a covering letter (March 30, 1973) was sent to the churches participating in the Preparatory Assembly. Strongly supporting the request of the two Assembly chairmen, Professor Max Geiger (Reformed) and Professor Marc Lienhard (Lutheran), the three staff officials expressed the conviction that "all further work must be undertaken in the closest possible contact with the churches themselves."

That the Leuenberg Agreement carries its message to churches in Asia, Africa, Australasia, and the Americas is readily evident. *Lutheran World* (20[1973]:347-53) here brings two documents: under A. instructions "To the Churches Participating in the Drafting of the Agreement" as to the next steps; and under B. the revised and received text of the Agreement.

A. TO THE CHURCHES PARTICIPATING IN THE DRAFTING OF THE AGREEMENT

On behalf of the "Preparatory Assembly for the Drafting of an Agreement between the Reformation Churches in Europe," and in accordance with its decision, we are sending you herewith the final text of the Agreement between the Reformation churches in Europe as revised at the Preparatory Assembly's second meeting from March 12-16, 1973, with the request that the church should take the necessary steps to reach a decision on the acceptance of the Agreement.

1. The European churches having noted the Schauenburg Theses (1967) and being largely in agreement with them, at their express wish and with their direct participation the so-called "Leuenberg Conversations" were held (1969-1970). The main theme of these conversations was the question of church fellowship. The churches' official representatives at these conversations recommended that work be begun on drafting an Agreement which could form the basis for achieving church fellowship. Having noted and approved this recommendation, the churches appointed their delegates for the drafting of the text of an Agreement. Meeting in Leuenberg from September 19-24, 1971, the official delegates of the churches produced the draft of an Agreement between the Reformation churches of Europe.

2. In September, 1971, the Preparatory Assembly set up a Continuation Committee which made preparations for the second meeting of the Preparatory Assembly in March, 1973. In accordance with its mandate, the Continuation Committee held several meetings

to consider the replies received from the churches, and proposed a revised version of the text of the Agreement. In respect of the requests of a few churches, the Continuation Committee itself was unable to establish a final text of the Agreement. At its second meeting, the Preparatory Assembly had before it a report from the Continuation Committee as well as the Committee's written proposals for changes in the text of the Agreement. It also received and considered a synopsis of the replies from the churches, together with a number of comments from church groups and individuals. Up to that time, replies had been received from 63 churches, and a further 9 churches were able to inform the Assembly about their preliminary discussions by means of detailed documents, even although their final answers were still not completed.

3. It was with thankfulness and joy that the Preparatory Assembly discovered that the churches represented in it were practically unanimous in their resolve to continue to seek church fellowship between the Reformation churches of Europe on the basis of an agreement. This was all the more remarkable because many of the churches, in determining their official response, had not only taken into account the views of professional theologians and university faculties but had also to a large extent drawn their ordained ministers and congregations into the process of reaching a common mind.

4. In the light of its study of the comments received, the Preparatory Assembly decided to base all its further work and decisions on this unanimity of the churches in approving the choice of an Agreement as the goal and the method to be pursued. It became convinced that, once the text had been revised, what could be done had been done, and that its work had therefore come to its conclusion. It believes that the matter would not be furthered substantially were the churches invited to comment again, and it therefore now requests the participant churches to accept the Agreement.

5. Important changes suggested have been incorporated in this revised text, and as far as possible a number of basic questions have been clarified.

Wherever possible, the language of the draft text has been improved in response to the criticisms expressed in some of the replies. It should, of course, be borne in mind that the doctrinal differences, which it was the purpose of the Agreement to overcome, are formulated in the characteristic language of the confessions or traditions. In dealing with these verbal formulations of doctrine, therefore, it was necessary to employ a corresponding style. The Preparatory Assembly was fully aware that the task of finding a contemporary language still confronts the churches, and must be tackled in the continuing doctrinal discussions.

In revising the text, care was taken not to add any new propositions. The Agreement does not need to treat every subject dealt with in the confessions and traditions of the individual churches. But it was also essential not to tighten and abbreviate the text to the detriment of the common understanding of the gospel which is required as the basis of the church fellowship into which the churches are to enter. After full discussion the Preparatory Assembly decided that a short form of declaration, giving just a brief account of the consensus which exists between the churches, would not suffice for an affirmation of church fellowship.

6. The Procedure for the Reception

a) The text of the Agreement between the Reformation churches of Europe adopted by the second Preparatory Assembly is attested by the signatures of the four chairmen of the Preparatory Assembly, namely, Dr. Max Geiger of Basle, Dr. Leonhard Goppelt of Munich, Dr. Horst Lahr of Potsdam, and Dr. Marc Lienhard of Strasbourg. The signed document is deposited with the World Council of Churches, and copies of it with the Lutheran World Federation and the World Alliance of Reformed Churches.

b) The participant churches are invited to indicate their assent in writing by September 30, 1974.

c) The following declaration should be included in the written assent: "The . . . (name of the church) . . . assents to the version of the Agreement between the Reformation churches of Europe (the Leuenberg Agreement) adopted on March 16, 1973."

d) Declarations of assent should be sent to the World Council of Churches (Faith and Order Commission, 150 route de Ferney, 1211 Geneva 20, Switzerland) where they will be deposited. Participant churches will be informed of each declaration of assent received by the World Council of Churches.

e) Church fellowship in the sense indicated in the Agreement will come into effect on October 1, 1974, between those churches whose declaration of assent has then been received by the World Council of Churches.

f) Churches whose declaration of assent reaches the World Council of Churches after September 30, 1974, will be participants in church fellowship in the sense indicated in the Agreement from the date on which their declaration is received.

7. The Preparatory Assembly made the following proposals concerning the achievement of church fellowship.

a) The participant churches are asked to send in suggestions and requests concerning the practical realization of church fellowship, together with subjects for the proposed continuing doctrinal conversations.

b) If possible, these doctrinal conversations should be initiated still in 1974. Invitations to participate in them will be sent even to those churches which have not yet been able to reach a decision to assent to the Agreement by the time the doctrinal discussions are resumed. The Continuation Committee will discuss detailed arrangements with the Lutheran World Federation and the World Alliance of Reformed Churches.

c) The Preparatory Assembly came to the opinion that the calling of a "General Assembly" as envisaged in earlier letters can for the present be disregarded. This does not exclude the possibility of calling a General Assembly at a date to be specified later, if the participant churches consider this desirable. It could, for example, take place in conjunction with the beginning of the continuing doctrinal discussions.

8. The Continuation Committee appointed by the Preparatory Assembly consists of the following members: Professor Dr. Andreas Aarflot (Professor Dr. Holsten Faberberg); Bishop Helge Brattgård

(Professor Dr. Fredric Cleve); The Rev. Martin H. Cressey (The Rev. Professor Allan D. Galloway); Professor Dr. Wilhelm Dantine (Prelate Dr. Albrecht Hege); Bishop Dr. Emerich Varga (Pastor Johan A. Dvoracek); Professor Dr. Max Geiger (Professor Dr. Louis Rumpf); Professor Dr. Leonhard Goppelt (Bishop Dr. Friedrich Hübner); Oberkirchenrat (retired) Dr. Karl Herberg (Prelate Dr. Hans Bornhäuser); Pastor Attila Kovach (Pastor G. Gyula Röhrig); General Superintendent Dr. Horst Lahr (Oberkirchenrat Dr. Werner Tannert); Professor Dr. Marc Lienhard (Pastor Alain Blancy); Oberkirchenrat Olav Lingner (Oberkirchenrat Dr. Werner Hofmann); Professor Dr. Wenzel Lohff (Dr. Hans Martin Müller); Dr. Remko J. Mooi (Professor Dr. Daniel Vidal); Dr. Paolo Ricca; President Hugo Schnell (Oberkirchenrat Hermann Greifenstein); Praeses Professor Dr. Joachim Staedtke (Landessuperintendent Dr. Gerhard Nordholt).

It is the responsibility of the Continuation Committee to carry out the tasks mentioned in paragraphs 6 and 7.

Signed on behalf of the Preparatory Assembly.

Professor Dr. Max Geiger, *Chairman*

Professor Dr. Marc Lienhard, *Chairman*

B. AGREEMENT BETWEEN REFORMATION CHURCHES IN EUROPE (LEUENBERG AGREEMENT)

(1) On the basis of their doctrinal discussions, the churches assenting to this Agreement—namely, Lutheran and Reformed churches in Europe along with the Union churches which grew out of them, and the related pre-Reformation churches, the Waldensian Church and the Church of the Czech Brethren—affirm together the common understanding of the gospel elaborated below. This common understanding of the gospel enables them to declare and to realize church fellowship. Thankful that they have been led closer together, they confess at the same time that guilt and suffering have also accompanied and still accompany the struggle for truth and unity in the church.

(2) The church is founded upon Jesus Christ alone. It is he who gathers the church and sends it forth, by the bestowal of his salvation in preaching and the sacraments. In the view of the Reformation, it follows that agreement in the right teaching of the gospel, and in the right administration of the sacraments, is the necessary and sufficient prerequisite for the true unity of the church. It is from these Reformation criteria that the participating churches derive their view of church fellowship as set out below.

I. The Road to Fellowship

(3) Faced with real differences in style of theological thinking and church practice, the fathers of the Reformation, despite much that they had in common, did not see themselves in a position, on grounds of faith and conscience, to avoid divisions. In this Agreement the participating churches acknowledge that their relationship to one another has changed since the time of the Reformation.

1. Common Aspects at the Outset of the Reformation

(4) With the advantage of historical distance, it is easier today to discern the common elements in the witness of the churches of the Reformation, in spite of the differences between them: "Their starting point was a new experience of the power of the gospel to liberate and assure. In standing up for the truth which they saw, the Reformers found themselves drawn together in opposition to the church traditions of that time. They were, therefore, at one in confessing that the church's life and doctrine are to be gauged by the original and pure testimony to the gospel in Scripture. They were at one in bearing witness to God's free and unconditional grace in the life, death, and resurrection of Jesus Christ for all those who believe this promise. They were at one in confessing that the practice and form of the church should be determined only by the commission to deliver this testimony to the world, and that the word of God remains sovereign over every human ordering of the Christian community. In so doing, they were at one with the whole of Christendom

in receiving and renewing the confession of the triune God and the God-manhood of Jesus Christ as expressed in the ancient creeds of the church.

2. Changed Elements in the Contemporary Situation

(5) In the course of 400 years of history, the churches of the Reformation have been led to new and similar ways of thinking and living: by theological wrestling with the questions of modern times, by advances in biblical research, by the movements of church renewal, and by the rediscovery of the ecumenical horizon. These developments certainly have also brought with them new differences cutting right across the confessions. But, time and again, there has also been an experience of brotherly fellowship, particularly in times of common suffering. The result of all these factors was a new concern on the part of the churches, especially since the revival movement, to achieve a contemporary expression both of the biblical witness and of the Reformation confessions of faith. In the process they have learned to distinguish between the fundamental witness of the Reformation confessions of faith and their historically conditioned thought forms. Because these confessions of faith bear witness to the gospel as the living word of God in Jesus Christ, far from barring the way to continued responsible testimony to the Word, they open up this way with a summons to follow it in the freedom of faith.

II. The Common Understanding of the Gospel

(6) In what follows, the participating churches describe their common understanding of the gospel insofar as this is required for establishing church fellowship between them.

1. The Message of Justification as the Message of the Free Grace of God

(7) The gospel is the message of Jesus Christ, the salvation of the world, in fulfillment of the promise given to the people of the Old Covenant.

(8) a) The true understanding of the gospel was expressed by fathers of the Reformation in the doctrine of justification.

(9) b) In this message, Jesus Christ is acknowledged as the one in whom God became man and bound himself to man; as the crucified and risen one who took God's judgment upon himself and, in so doing, demonstrated God's love to sinners; and as the coming one who, as Judge and Savior, leads the world to its consummation.

(10) c) Through his word, God by his Holy Spirit calls all men to repent and believe, and assures the believing sinner of his righteousness in Jesus Christ. Whoever puts his trust in the gospel is justified in God's sight for the sake of Jesus Christ, and set free from the accusation of the law. In daily repentance and renewal, he lives within the fellowship in praise of God and in service to others, in the assurance that God will bring his kingdom in all its fulness. In this way, God creates new life, and plants in the midst of the world the seed of a new humanity.

(11) d) This message sets Christians free for responsible service in the world and makes them ready to suffer in this service. They know that God's will, as demand and succour, embraces the whole world. They stand up for temporal justice and peace between individuals and nations. To do this they have to join with others in seeking rational and appropriate criteria, and play their part in applying these criteria. They do so in the confidence that God sustains the world and as those who are accountable to him.

(12) e) In this understanding of the gospel, we take our stand on the basis of the ancient creeds of the church, and reaffirm the common conviction of the Reformation confessions that the unique mediation of Jesus Christ in salvation is the heart of the Scriptures, and the message of justification as the message of God's free grace is the measure of all the church's preaching.

2. Preaching, Baptism, and the Lord's Supper

(13) The fundamental witness to the gospel is the testimony of the apostles and prophets in the Holy Scriptures of the Old and New Testaments. It is the task of the church to spread this gospel by the

spoken word in preaching, by individual counselling, and by baptism and the Lord's Supper. In preaching, baptism, and the Lord's Supper, Jesus Christ is present through the Holy Spirit. Justification in Christ is thus imparted to men, and in this way the Lord gathers his people. In doing so he employs various forms of ministry and service, as well as the witness of all those belonging to his people.

a) Baptism

14) Baptism is administered in the name of the Father and of the Son and of the Holy Spirit with water. In baptism, Jesus Christ irrevocably receives man, fallen prey to sin and death, into his fellowship of salvation so that he may become a new creature. In the power of his Holy Spirit, he calls him into his community and to a new life of faith, to daily repentance, and to discipleship.

b) The Lord's Supper

(15) In the Lord's Supper the risen Christ imparts himself in his body and blood, given up for all, through his word of promise with bread and wine. He thereby grants us forgiveness of sins, and sets us free for a new life of faith. He enables us to experience anew that we are members of his body. He strengthens us for service to all men.

(16) When we celebrate the Lord's Supper we proclaim the death of Christ through which God has reconciled the world with himself. We proclaim the presence of the risen Lord in our midst. Rejoicing that the Lord has come to us, we await his future coming in glory.

III. Accord in Respect of the Doctrinal Condemnations of the Reformation Era

(17) The differences which from the time of the Reformation onwards have made church fellowship between Lutheran and Reformed churches impossible, and have led them to pronounce mutual condemnations, relate to the doctrine of the Lord's Supper, christology, and the doctrine of predestination. We take the decisions of

the Reformation fathers seriously, but are today able to agree on the following statements in respect of these condemnations:

1. The Lord's Supper

(18) In the Lord's Supper the risen Jesus Christ imparts himself in his body and blood, given up for all, through his word of promise with bread and wine. He thus gives himself unreservedly to all who receive the bread and wine; faith receives the Lord's Supper for salvation, unfaith for judgment.

(19) We cannot separate communion with Jesus Christ in his body and blood from the act of eating and drinking. To be concerned about the manner of Christ's presence in the Lord's Supper in abstraction from this act is to run the risk of obscuring the meaning of the Lord's Supper.

(20) Where such a consensus exists between the churches, the condemnations pronounced by the Reformation confessions are inapplicable to the doctrinal position of these churches.

2. Christology

(21) In the true man Jesus Christ, the eternal Son, and so God himself, has bestowed himself upon lost mankind for its salvation. In the word of the promise and in the sacraments, the Holy Spirit, and so God himself, makes the crucified and risen Jesus present to us.

(22) Believing in this self-bestowal of God in his Son, the task facing us, in view of the historically conditioned character of traditional thought forms, is to give renewed and effective expression to the special insights of the Reformed tradition, with its concern to maintain unimpaired the divinity and humanity of Jesus, and to those of the Lutheran tradition, with its concern to maintain the unity of Jesus as a person.

(23) In these circumstances, it is impossible for us to reaffirm the former condemnations today.

3. Predestination

(24) In the gospel we have the promise of God's unconditional acceptance of sinful man. Whoever puts his trust in the gospel can know that he is saved, and praise God for his election. For this reason we can speak of election only with respect to the call to salvation in Christ.

(25) Faith knows by experience that the message of salvation is not accepted by all; yet it respects the mystery of God's dealings with men. It bears witness to the seriousness of human decisions, and at the same time to the reality of God's universal purpose of salvation. The witness of the Scriptures to Christ forbids us to suppose that God has uttered an eternal decree for the final condemnation of specific individuals or of a particular people.

(26) When such a consensus exists between churches, the condemnations pronounced by the Reformation confessions of faith are inapplicable to the doctrinal position of these churches.

4. Conclusions

(27) Wherever these statements are accepted, the condemnations of the Reformation confessions in respect of the Lord's Supper, christology, and predestination are inapplicable to the doctrinal position. This does not mean that the condemnations pronounced by the Reformation fathers are irrelevant; but they are no longer an obstacle to church fellowship.

(28) There remain considerable differences between our churches in forms of worship, types of spirituality, and church order. These differences are often more deeply felt in the congregations than the traditional doctrinal differences. Nevertheless, in fidelity to the New Testament and Reformation criteria for church fellowship, we cannot discern in these differences any factors which should divide the church.

IV. The Declaration and Realization of Church Fellowship

(29) In the sense intended in this Agreement, church fellowship means that, on the basis of the consensus they have reached in their understanding of the gospel, churches with different confessional positions accord each other fellowship in word and sacrament, and strive for the fullest possible cooperation in witness and service to the world.

1. Declaration of Church Fellowship

(30) In assenting to this Agreement the churches, in loyalty to the confessions of faith which bind them, or with due respect for their traditions, declare:

(31) a) that they are one in understanding the gospel as set out in Parts II and III;

(32) b) that, in accordance with what is said in Part III, the doctrinal condemnations expressed in the confessional documents no longer apply to the contemporary doctrinal position of the assenting churches;

(33) c) that they accord each other table and pulpit fellowship; this includes the mutual recognition of ordination and the freedom to provide for intercelebration.

(34) With these statements, church fellowship is declared. The divisions which have barred the way to this fellowship since the 16th century are removed. The participating churches are convinced that they have been put together in the one church of Jesus Christ, and that the Lord liberates them for, and lays upon them the obligation of, common service.

2. Realizing Church Fellowship

(35) It is in the life of the churches and congregations that church fellowship becomes a reality. Believing in the unifying power of the Holy Spirit, they bear their witness and perform their service

together, and strive to deepen and strengthen the fellowship they have found together.

a) Witness and Service

(36) The preaching of the churches gains credibility in the world when they are at one in their witness to the gospel. The gospel liberates and binds together the churches to render common service. Being the service of love, it turns to man in his distress and seeks to remove the causes of that distress. The struggle for justice and peace in the world increasingly demands of the churches the acceptance of a common responsibility.

b) The Continuing Theological Task

(37) The Agreement leaves intact the binding force of the confessions within the participating churches. It is not to be regarded as a new confession of faith. It sets forth a consensus reached about central matters; one which makes church fellowship possible between churches of different confessional positions. In accordance with this consensus, the participating churches will seek to establish a common witness and service, and pledge themselves to their common doctrinal discussions.

(38) The common understanding of the gospel on which church fellowship is based must be further deepened, tested in the light of the witness of Holy Scripture, and continually made relevant in the contemporary scene.

(39) The churches have the task of studying further these differences of doctrine which, while they do not have divisive force, still persist within and between the participating churches. These include: hermeneutical questions concerning the understanding of Scripture, confession of faith, and church; the relation between law and gospel; baptismal practice; ministry and ordination; the "two kingdom" doctrine, and the doctrine of the sovereignty of Christ; and church and society. At the same time newly emerging problems relating to witness and service, order and practice, have to be considered.

(40) On the basis of their common heritage, the churches of the Reformation must determine their attitude to trends toward the theological polarization increasingly in evidence today. To some

extent the problems here go beyond the doctrinal differences which were once at the basis of the Lutheran–Reformed controversy.

(41) It will be the task of common theological study to testify to the truth of the gospel and to distinguish it from all distortions.

c) Organizational consequences

(42) This declaration of church fellowship does not anticipate provisions of church law on particular matters of inter-church relations, or within the churches. The churches will, however, take the Agreement into account considering such provisions.

(43) As a general rule, the affirmation of pulpit and table fellowship and the mutual recognition of ordination do not affect the rules in force in the participating churches for induction to a pastoral charge, the exercise of the pastoral ministry, or the ordering of congregational life.

(44) The question of organic union between particular participating churches can only be decided in the situation in which these churches live. In examining this question the following points should be kept in mind:

(45) Any union detrimental to the lively plurality in styles of preaching, ways of worship, church order, and in diaconal and social action, would contradict the very nature of the church fellowship inaugurated by this declaration. On the other hand, in certain situations, because of the intimate connection between witness and order, the church's service may call for formal legal unification. Where organizational consequences are drawn from this declaration, it should not be at the expense of freedom of decision in minority churches.

d) Ecumenical Aspects

(46) In establishing and realizing church fellowship among themselves, the participating churches do so as part of their responsibility to promote the ecumenical fellowship of all Christian churches.

(47) They regard such a fellowship of churches in the European area as a contribution to this end. They hope that the ending of their previous separation will influence churches in Europe and elsewhere

who are related to them confessionally. They are ready to examine with them the possibilities of wider church fellowship.

(48) This hope applies equally to the relationship between the Lutheran World Federation and the World Alliance of Reformed Churches.

(49) They also hope that the achievement of church fellowship with each other will provide a fresh stimulus to conference and cooperation with churches of other confessions. They affirm their readiness to set their doctrinal discussions within this wider context.